The Daily Telegraph

A–Z GUIDE TO
MOTORING LAW

Fenton Bresler has been in practice at the Bar for many years. Almost from the very beginning of his career he has also written extensively on the law in newspapers, magazines and books, and has contributed to television and radio programmes on the law. Currently, he has no fewer than seven regular columns in the national Press and on the Internet, including a monthly column on motoring law in the *Daily Telegraph*.

The Daily Telegraph

A–Z GUIDE TO
MOTORING LAW
FENTON BRESLER

MACMILLAN

First published 2001 by Macmillan
an imprint of Macmillan Publishers Ltd
25 Eccleston Place, London sw1w 9nf
Basingstoke and Oxford
Associated companies throughout the world
www.macmillan.com

In association with the *Daily Telegraph*

ISBN 0 333 90481 8

1 3 5 7 9 8 6 4 2

A CIP catalogue record for this book is available from
the British Library.

Typeset by SetSystems Ltd, Saffron Walden, Essex
Printed and bound in Great Britain by
Mackays of Chatham plc, Chatham, Kent

Contents

Acknowledgements

I must put on record my warm thanks to Peter Hall, *Daily Telegraph* Motoring Editor, and his team for their consistent support for my 'Street Legal' column over the years and to Susannah Charlton, Publisher Telegraph Books, who first suggested this book and has done so much to help bring it to fruition.

Introduction

Most of the 32 million qualified drivers in this country know very little about motoring law. They probably took their driving test years ago, and even the 5 million provisional licence holders who have not yet taken their test often cannot see the wood for the trees. There simply is so much law!

Ever since 1993 I have had a monthly column called 'Street Legal' in the *Daily Telegraph* in which, drawing upon over forty years of experience as a practising barrister, legal journalist and motorist, I have done my best to write knowledgeably and, I hope, interestingly on the subject of motoring law. An elderly barrister once dismissed me with a perceptible sniff as 'a populist'. I happily accept the title.

This book does not aim to be an encyclopaedic legal textbook but to address all those legal issues that the average motorist is likely to encounter in the course of a driving life. Whether we have driven for a long time or are still learners, we can all benefit from guidance when dealing with the sometimes bewildering complexities of motoring law. Back in the 1950s, Lord Goddard, then Lord Chief Justice, calculated that there were over 1,000 offences that a driver could commit. Nowadays, the figure could probably be at least trebled.

Motorists come into contact – and, all too frequently,

conflict – with the law more often than any other section of the community. They end up involved with the police and the courts more than any other normally law-abiding citizens and it is more likely to cost them hard-earned money by way of fine or fixed penalty, or paying for other methods of transport if they lose their licence through, for instance, drink-driving or a serious case of speeding.

This book will help you to keep out of avoidable trouble with the law and will tell you what your rights are, should you fall foul of it. It is primarily concerned with car drivers, but most of the following pages are also relevant for drivers of other motor vehicles and motor cycles. Although it is not possible to cover everything in a book of this size, you will find most of what you need for everyday purposes. This is a guide, not a legal textbook. But all knowledge is power, and this is nowhere more true than with motoring law.

Scotland has its own legal system but, although Scots should read 'sheriff' or 'district court' for magistrates' court, and 'Court of Session' for High Court, motoring law is much the same throughout the United Kingdom.

I have done my best to make the book as accurate as I can, and as up to date as I can at the time of going to press (in February 2001), but neither the publishers nor myself intend to render a professional service with this publication nor are we liable for any error or omission it may contain, for any use to which its contents are put or for any loss arising therefrom.

A

ACCIDENTS

What does the law say if you are unfortunate enough to have an accident while driving a car on a public road?

Section 170 of the 1988 Road Traffic Act contains most of the answer. It states that, irrespective of whether or not careless driving was involved or of who caused the accident, your first duty is to stop. Obviously you must use discretion: if possible, you should not stop in the middle of a busy road but should try to pull into the kerb. If another motorist is involved, he too must stop, but the police need only be called if someone has been injured. If not, your only obligation is, 'if required by any person having reasonable grounds to do so' (e.g. the other driver or the owner of damaged property), to give your name and address, those of the owner of the vehicle you are driving if it is not your own, and its registration number. Any other motorist involved is of course under the same obligation.

Many drivers think they are entitled to demand the other driver's driving licence and current insurance certificate; but Section 170 says nothing at all about a driving licence and stipulates that a motorist only has to show his insurance certificate if someone else – not only himself – has been injured.

Not every accident, however, brings with it the duty to stop and give particulars. That only applies when someone else (i.e. not merely yourself) is injured, when *another* vehicle (which includes a bicycle) or property is damaged, or when any animal (except a cat!) not being carried in your own car is injured. Because a cat is not an 'animal' as defined by Section 170, do not make the common mistake of thinking that you can drive on with impunity, should you injure one. If there is a reasonable chance of helping it, you should stop; otherwise, if you are spotted, you could be reported for causing it unnecessary suffering, contrary to the 1911 Protection of Animals Act – which does define a cat as an 'animal'.

Incidentally, an injured human being does not have the same legal protection. The only obligation imposed by Section 170, if you have injured or killed someone, is to call the police if particulars and insurance certificates have not been exchanged. There is sadly only a moral obligation to do any more, such as call an ambulance or try to find some other form of help. But what would you expect in a country that boasts a Royal Society for the Prevention of Cruelty to Animals but only a National Society for the Prevention of Cruelty to Children? (See **Hit and Run**.)

If you do not give particulars at the time of the accident, perhaps because there was no one there to ask (for instance, the absent owner of a damaged parked car), it is no defence to say no one was around. You should at least have left a note on the windscreen with your contact details. If, for whatever reason, particulars were not given at the time, you must report the accident at a police station or to a police officer 'as soon as reasonably practicable and in any case within twenty-four hours'.

The High Court has ruled, in *Bulman* v. *Bennett*, that those words mean exactly what they say. You must not put off reporting the accident for up to twenty-four hours: you must do it 'as soon as reasonably practicable'. Only if it is not possible to report the accident promptly do you have up to twenty-four hours in which to do so.

Furthermore, the High Court has also ruled, in *Wisdom* v. *Macdonald*, that you cannot simply telephone a police station to report. You must do so in person. Failure to stop and give particulars to anyone reasonably requiring them is one offence and failing to report to the police is another, separate offence. You could easily find yourself convicted of both. Neither is a laughing matter, for each carries a maximum six-month gaol sentence or £5,000 fine (although I know of no case where the offender has been punished so severely) and five to ten penalty points.

There are three qualifications to all this.

If you can convince a Bench of cynical magistrates that you genuinely did not know there had been an accident, the case will be thrown out. This is unlikely when there has been an accident on the open road but, where you are trying to manoeuvre in or out of tightly parked cars, it is not entirely impossible. Some years ago, the Queen's cousin Lord Harewood was acquitted at Bow Street Magistrates' Court in central London when he successfully claimed that he had not realized he had backed into a parked car because he was listening to a Mozart wind serenade on his car radio. He explained that he might have confused the sound of a burglar alarm, set off on the parked car, with a sustained note on the clarinet.

But there is a limit. In 1989, a driver tried to avoid being convicted of failing to report by saying he did not realize there had been a mishap until fifteen minutes later. It did him no good, however. The High Court ruled that a driver does not have to realize an accident has occurred *at the time*: later will do.

Section 170 used to apply only where the accident occurs 'on a road', and the 1988 Act gave a limited meaning to that deceptively simple word. It had to be a highway or 'other road to which the public has access'. It therefore did not include a private road or a car park. But the 2000 Motor Vehicles (Compulsory Insurance) Regulations has changed all that. It extends Section 170 to include 'public places', which comprise most car parks (see **Car Parks**).

Section 154 of the 1988 Act (coupled with the 2000 Regulations) says that anyone against whom a civil claim has actually been made arising out of their use of a motor vehicle on a road or in a public place is obliged to tell the claimant whether they were insured and, if they were, to give details of their insurance policy. It also states that anyone not doing so, without reasonable excuse, is 'guilty of an offence' for which they can be fined up to £2,500. But police enforcement is haphazard; some forces consider that this creates only a civil obligation and not a criminal offence. Perhaps the reluctance to prosecute stems from an attitude that it is 'only' wealthy insurance companies which are suffering. But that is nonsense. General claims losses are inevitably passed on to motorists in the form of increased premiums. In fact, it has been suggested that the lack of uniform enforcement of Section 154 costs the motor insurance industry millions of pounds each year.

ADVERTISING LEAFLETS

Many motorists find it a nuisance to come back to their car and find advertising leaflets put under their windscreen wipers – but is this activity an offence? As with many an apparently simple question in motoring law, the answer is far from simple.

For a start, it all depends on where your car is parked. If this is in a council car park, the answer is definitely 'Yes' – at least, ever since a High Court decision in October 1991. This upheld a conviction by magistrates in Chichester, West Sussex, of the owner of a local wine bar who had put leaflets advertising his establishment on windscreens in the city's Northgate car park. Chichester Council, concerned about its car parks becoming littered with discarded leaflets, brought a first prosecution under local by-laws similar to those in force in many other towns and cities.

What was the alleged offence? 'Using a vehicle, while it is in a [council] parking place, for any purpose in connection with trade or business', contrary to Article 15 of the Chichester (Off-street Parking Places) Order 1981.

But how could the defendant be 'using' a parked vehicle when he was only using a printed piece of paper – i. e. the leaflet? Surely the only person who can 'use' a motor vehicle is its driver? Mr Justice McCullough did not agree. 'One can use something without having any control over it. The person sleeping in a stranger's car provides one example. Others are those who use public transport . . . In my judgment,' he continued, 'the intention of Article 15 is to prohibit the promotion of trade or business from the presence of vehicles in parking places. For a contravention, the defendant must (i) use a vehicle for a business or trade purpose while it is in the parking place and (ii) *intend such purpose to be advanced by the presence of the vehicle in the parking place.*' The italics are mine. The meaning is that a tradesman's own vehicle parked in a council car park does not break the law, even though it advertises his name and address in large letters painted on the side, because that information is always there, not merely while the vehicle is in the car park. Putting advertising material on strangers' cars in a car park comes into a different category.

But what about people who put leaflets under the windscreen wipers of cars parked in the street or in private car parks? Do they also commit an offence? In private car parks, they commit, at the very least, a civil trespass and could be banned from the car park. But in the street they almost certainly do not commit an offence – although no one, in the current state of the law, can be absolutely sure.

I can point to no generally known by-law – or national law, such as the 1988 or 1991 Road Traffic Act – to solve the problem. Owners of residents' council parking permits may commit an offence by allowing their vehicle to be used for trade purposes while parked in a residents' parking bay – but that does not make it unlawful for someone else to do so.

There is, however, one new possibility. In London recently, one of the new breed of inner-city young men who intimidate motorists into handing over money for washing their windscreen while their car is waiting at traffic lights (see **Windscreen Cleaners**) was, at Marylebone Magistrates' Court, found guilty of street trading without a licence, contrary to the 1990 London Local Authorities Act. He was fined £30 with £70 costs.

Could putting advertising literature under windscreen wipers be equated with windscreen washing, so as to amount to 'street trading'? I can see arguments for and against that proposition. Chichester Council made new law for council off-street car parking throughout the country in October 1991. Now another public-spirited council could bring a second test case for on-street parking for London and other cities with similar street trading laws. Are there any takers?

AGE

We all know that elderly motorists can be ordered to retake the driving test, but when does this happen and is there a specified legal age?

To answer the second question first: there is no specified age. An Automobile Association (AA) spokesman once depressed me immeasurably by telling me that any driver

over fifty-five is considered 'elderly'. He explained: 'That
is the youngest age at which medical research shows that
our physical reactions begin to slow down, to however
small an extent.'

But that is not the view of the law. There are four
minimum ages at which, with a valid licence and having
passed the driving test, you can ride or drive a motor
vehicle on a public road.[1] These are: sixteen for a moped
or invalid carriage; seventeen for a car, van, motorcycle up
to 25 kW (33 bhp) or farm tractor; eighteen for a medium-
sized goods vehicle; and twenty-one for all other kinds of
motor vehicle (including any size of motorcycle, with or
without a sidecar, and a bus!). But there is no maximum
age at which you must either retake the test or give up
driving. A case some years ago in which an eighty-six-
year-old woman had a fatal heart attack at the wheel of
her car, killing a young mother and critically injuring a
four-month-old baby, caused some people concern about
the law as it applies to elderly drivers. There were several
Press reports that the Department of the Environment,
Transport and the Regions (DETR) was actively considering new regulations requiring all motorists to retake the
driving test on reaching a specified age – but nothing came
of it.

Competent elderly drivers can put their minds at rest.
So long as they believe that they are still sufficiently
mentally and physically alert to go on driving, the law

1 On private roads and private land, there is no minimum age. But if a
   youngster's inexperience or incompetence causes injury or damage, they
   – and the person allowing them to drive – can be sued for compensation.

allows them to do so. Indeed, statistics bear out that young, careless drivers are much more likely to have an accident than elderly, careful motorists.

The only legal age-mark is that fifty-six days before your seventieth birthday when your normal driving licence is due to expire (see **Driving Licence**), the Driving and Vehicle Licensing Agency (DVLA) at Swansea will send a computerized application form for a new three-year licence to your last known address. This will include a medical questionnaire asking you to disclose any new physical disabilities, such as giddiness or worsening eyesight. Most people put 'None', sign the form, send it off together with a £8.50 renewal fee, get their new licence and then go on happily repeating the process every three years (the EU thinks this should be reduced to two years) for as long as they want to go on driving.

But no one verifies the answers. There are no regular medical check-ups for drivers on reaching a certain age. If you answer the questions truthfully and disclose a disability, you may then be asked to submit to a medical examination or produce your doctor's medical records. Otherwise nothing happens. It is entirely a matter of how honest you are. Your doctor does not have to sign the form. Views may differ as to whether this is satisfactory.

The decision whether – or when – to give up driving is a personal one, and can sometimes be difficult. As the AA spokesman said, 'Nowadays people want to hold on to their cars longer. There are a lot more elderly drivers – about seven million – on the roads and that number is expected at least to double over the next thirty years.'

Yet even advanced old age need not be decisive. My own mother-in-law was still driving at ninety-one without ever having had an accident – or, indeed, ever having taken the driving test. She was already driving when the darned thing was introduced! But she was an intelligent woman and selective when and where she drove; she never went out at night on busy roads.

That is to be contrasted with the eighty-two-year-old chartered accountant who pleaded guilty to careless driving at Abingdon, Oxfordshire, and was fined £175, disqualified for a year, and ordered to retake his test if he still wanted to drive at the end of that time. Despite wearing a hearing-aid and glasses, he had an unblemished record stretching back sixty years. But on a darkening January evening he had become confused when trying to find a route avoiding roadworks and had travelled 17 miles the wrong way down the A34 dual carriageway. 'This was not a wicked piece of driving. He was dazed, confused and in obvious shock,' said his lawyer.

That is exactly the sort of case in which a court is likely to use its discretionary power under Section 36 of the 1988 Road Traffic Offenders Act to disqualify offenders until they pass 'the appropriate driving test', i.e. a repeat of the standard 'L' test they had taken when starting to drive. This does not happen at random. The motorist must first be convicted of an offence for which his licence is endorsed: i.e. most major driving offences. If an elderly person does not commit such an offence, their licence is safe.

Furthermore, Section 36 says nothing specifically about age. It merely states that a court 'shall have regard to the safety of road users'. As Mr Justice Boreham commented in June 1990, when the Appeal Court upheld a retesting order on a thirty-four-year-old Essex sales representative convicted of a particularly unpleasant piece of reckless driving at night on the M11 motorway, 'He needs to be taught the lesson that a driver shall have proper regard for other road users.'

Arrogant, aggressive drivers, of whatever age, are at greater risk than competent older drivers. As Mr Justice Talbot said in January 1975 in *R. v. Donnelly*, 'This is not a punitive power but should be used in respect of people who are growing old or infirm or show some incompetence in the offence which needs looking into.'

In many cases, when a truly elderly person – and I mean someone in their late seventies or early eighties – is involved in a driving mishap which may cause them to be charged with an offence, they voluntarily surrender their licence before the case ever gets to court. They know themselves that they have reached the stage when 'Enough is enough'. For Britain's oldest driver, see **Elderly Drivers**.

ALARMS

The law gets into absolutely everything – including what Regulation 99 of the 1986 Road Vehicles (Construction and Use) Regulations calls 'a horn (not being a two-tone horn), bell, gong or siren to raise alarm as to the theft or attempted theft of the vehicle or its contents'. Those living or working in the vicinity of an activated car alarm will be glad to know that it must be fitted with a device which automatically cuts it out after five minutes. If not, there is a maximum fine, in theory, of £1,000 but prosecutions are seldom brought and usually the fine is less than one-tenth of that figure. If a car alarm in your street sounds for longer than five minutes, you would be within your rights in calling the police to come and de-activate it, on the grounds that it is not only breaching the Regulations but also causing a breach of the peace. (Incidentally, most motor insurers will give their customers a discount on their premium if they have a car alarm fitted.)

AMBULANCES

Rule 194 of the Highway Code spells out what the ordinary motorist is to do if he hears or sees an ambulance (or other emergency vehicle) approaching: 'Do not panic. Consider the route of the emergency vehicle and take appropriate action to let it pass. If necessary, pull to the side of the road and stop, but do not endanger other road users.' Failing to do this could lead to a charge of careless driving. See **Careless Driving** and **Highway Code**.

ANIMALS

Surprisingly, although there are strict legal provisions as to carrying children in cars (see **Children**), the law is silent about carrying animals. In fact, a friend of mine had a few unpleasant moments when her husband was driving her along the A41 in their family car and one of their two cats got out of its carrier on the back seat and jumped on to the inside of the front windscreen. Luckily she was able to grab hold of it and put it back into its carrier. But if a police officer had spotted them, her husband could have been booked for not being in proper control of their motor vehicle (see **Proper Control**). The moral is to ensure that any animal passenger is kept suitably restrained.

AUCTIONS

An auction is not the safest place to buy a used vehicle; although you may get one cheaper than from a dealer, you have far less legal protection. The written terms and conditions which you have to accept if you want to do business at the auction largely protect both the auction house and the seller from liability for any defects. If you are buying direct from a dealer, he cannot exclude his legal obligation under the 1979 Sale of Goods Act, as amended, to sell you a vehicle that is in 'satisfactory' condition, but the Act does not apply to auction houses or dealers selling at auctions. So it is little wonder that the AA warns in its leaflet *Buying a Used Car*: 'Auctions offer many bargains but, if you have little or no knowledge of cars, steer clear. Well-maintained ex-fleet cars are very attractive but mileage clocking (turning back the odometer to disguise the true mileage) and bad accident repair mean some shady pasts.' Furthermore, most auction-house terms and conditions only give a buyer until the end of the day's trading to obtain a refund for any misdescription. This is often far too soon for the buyer to discover the truth – as where a car was described as 'having no major mechanical faults' and at first seemed in good order, but after two weeks the buyer discovered that it needed substantial repairs, including work to the steering. These cost more than £700 – and he had to foot the bill himself.

B

BANS

As we shall see when discussing specific offences (see under **Dangerous Driving** or **Breath Tests**), and as all motorists know anyway, a court can take away your licence and ban you from driving for a stated length of time, if you are convicted of a major offence. As we also know, the same applies if you have accumulated too many penalty points in any one three-year period (see **Penalty Points** and **Totting Up**). But not everyone realizes that you can also be banned if convicted of speeding – the one offence that most of us are likely to commit. But when exactly is this likely to happen?

The 1988 Road Traffic Offenders Act, which lays down the penalties for speeding, is of no help at all. It states that you can be fined up to £1,000 and must have your licence endorsed with three to six penalty points, but that disqualification – the legal term for 'ban' – is merely 'discretionary'. What does this mean? The Act gives no guidelines as to how magistrates' courts, which alone deal with these cases, are to exercise their discretion. So the Magistrates' Association has resorted to self-help.

In its sentencing guidelines to members nationwide over the whole spectrum of criminal activity, it includes a section on speeding, although the Association emphasizes that its 'suggestions' are to be used only as a starting-point. Benches are advised to 'consider disqualification if 30 mph over limit', whatever that limit may be. So someone travelling at more than 60 mph in a built-up area where the speed limit is 30 mph is as likely to lose his licence for a short while as someone travelling at more than 100 mph on a motorway where, of course, the speed limit is 70 mph.

A Conservative MP once found this out the hard way. He was banned from driving for fourteen days (and fined £800 under the old, infamous unit fine system, where magistrates had little discretion in fixing the amount, and ordered to pay £100 costs) for entering the Norfolk village of Scole at 78 mph, although the police conceded that he had slowed to 65 mph while driving through the village itself. His period of disqualification fell exactly within the guidelines: 30–34 mph over the limit – six penalty points, £210 fine and a seven-day ban; 35–39 mph over the limit – six penalty points, £240 fine and a fourteen-day ban. But when the speed is 40 mph or more over the limit (e.g. 70 mph in a 30-mph area or 110 mph on a motorway), magistrates are recommended to show 'a sharp increase' in penalty and disqualification, with a minimum of twenty-one days.

When it comes to pleading guilty in a magistrates' court for speeding, most of us are at risk. Even two members of the Royal Family, Prince Michael of Kent and Viscount Linley, have lost their licences for short periods for speeding, and there have been many other examples involving well-known people.

For instance, Oscar-winning actor Daniel Day-Lewis was banned for seven days for driving his motorcycle at an average of 102.56 mph along the M5 on his way to catch a ferry. 'He wishes to apologize to all concerned,' his lawyer told magistrates in Cullompton, Devon.

Former pop singer and later financial guru Adam Faith was fined £800 and banned for twenty-one days for speeding at 110 mph on the M1. 'The court had no choice,' he said afterwards. 'I went too fast and got caught. It will make me think twice in future.'

BREATH TESTS

Forget all those crazy defences about offering a delicate part of the male anatomy for a blood test or taking a swig of whisky from a hip-flask so that the police cannot get an accurate alcohol reading. Those old legal loopholes have now long gone.

The 1988 Road Traffic Act states firmly that if a motorist drinks and drives – or even attempts to drive – he faces, if caught, almost certain disqualification by a magistrates' court (at least twelve months for a first offender, and often three times as long for a second offender), a maximum £5,000 fine and, in a really bad case, up to six months in prison.

Apart from the obvious dangers for the motorist and other people, drinking and driving simply are not worth the risk, even if mercifully no one is injured. Let me spell it out:

How much alcohol are you allowed to drink before driving?

This is the question that lawyers are most often asked – and there is no universal answer. It depends upon your individual metabolism. What the law *does* say is that anyone driving or attempting to drive a motor vehicle on a road or any other public place commits an offence if they have more than 35 micrograms (µg) of alcohol in 100 millilitres (ml) of breath, 80 milligrams (mg) of alcohol in 100 ml of blood, or 107 mg of alcohol in 100 ml of urine. It is misleading to try to express these limits in terms of glasses of wine/measures of spirits/pints of beer as so much depends on your size, your state of health and how used you are to drinking. Soon after the drink-driving laws were first introduced in the 1967 Road Safety Act, a leading forensic scientist, the late Dr Keith Simpson, told me, 'Don't drink and drive but when you aren't driving, keep in practice with your drinking!'

What is 'any other public place'?

This includes public-house car parks. You can be stopped and breath-tested here before you even reach the road.

When can you be stopped?

A police officer in uniform, but not in plain clothes, can stop and ask you for a roadside breath test if he reasonably suspects you of having some alcohol in your body. He does not have to believe you are over the limit. But you must first have committed a moving traffic offence, however slight, or had an accident. Many police forces nowadays breath-test every driver involved in an accident, even the innocent party.

What about random breath tests?

When breath tests were introduced in 1967, random testing was supposed to be illegal. But the police can still lie in wait outside public houses and stop motorists, even without a moving traffic offence or accident. And they can legally test you if they then smell alcohol on your breath.

This is because, back in December 1972, in the High Court case of *Harris* v. *Croson*, Lord Widgery, then Lord Chief Justice, ruled that a uniformed police officer can stop a motorist at any time. If he then happens to smell alcohol on the driver's breath, he can test him. This ruling has given the police a wonderful way, if they are so minded, of getting around the ban on random testing.

What if you manage to get home ahead of the police?

Many drivers think that gives them sanctuary but they are wrong. If you have had an accident in which someone else has been hurt, a uniformed officer can enter your home by force, if necessary, and request a breath test. But he must explain why. If he pushes his way in, demanding a test without giving an explanation, the local magistrates' court may later rule that this behaviour has been 'oppressive' and dismiss the case – even if you were over the limit (see also **Home**).

What happens if you refuse a breath test?
Doing so without reasonable cause is, in itself, an offence carrying a maximum £1,000 fine, four penalty points and disqualification. You will be arrested and taken to a police station. So you have only brought more trouble upon yourself!

What happens at the police station?
If the roadside breath test has proved positive or you have been arrested for refusing, you will be asked for a specimen of breath for instant analysis on an officially approved device known as an intoximeter; and you cannot gain time by asking for a lawyer. You must give two specimens and the print-out is immediate. But there are three safeguards: only the lower reading is used; the police will usually drop the matter if the lower reading is less than 40 µg; if under 50 µg, or if the station has no intoximeter available, the police must offer you an alternative test of blood or urine if they wish to be sure of getting a conviction in the event of that further test proving positive.

If, in the last instance, they do not give you the choice and both breath readings are only just over the lower limit, an experienced defence lawyer may be able to get the case dropped without going to court. As a solicitor reader of the *Daily Telegraph* has written to me, he got this result in a case where the readings were 41 and 40 µg.

When blood or urine is offered, the police, *not* the motorist, has the ultimate choice. But blood can only be taken by a police doctor and the police must ask if there is any reason against it. When a constable ignored a driver's reply, 'I'm taking tablets', the subsequent conviction was overturned on appeal because the police officer should have asked for more information.

When can you refuse a breath test or blood analysis?

Only if you are physically or mentally unable to give the specimen or if it would entail a substantial risk to your health – which you would later have to prove in court.

When can you cite a medical reason for not giving blood?

The High Court has pronounced on this vexed issue which can arise in two possible situations.

Either a roadside breath test has proved positive and the suspect has been arrested but no officially approved device for taking a conclusive breath specimen is available at the police station. *Or* such a device is available and has been used but the result is only marginal, showing more than 35 µg of alcohol in 100 ml of breath (the legal limit) but less than 50 µg.

In those circumstances, the 1988 Road Traffic Act states that the police must offer the motorist the choice of giving a specimen of either blood or urine – which the police have the right to select.

So much is crystal clear. But, in cases going right up to the House of Lords, the judges have put a gloss on the statute – and muddied its simple provisions – by ruling that the police officer must warn the motorist that not providing the specimen is an offence and that, if the officer decides to require blood, he must tell the motorist that the only right to object is for medical reasons which will have to be determined by the police doctor.

The lawfulness of the blood test – or of any refusal to give blood – will then turn upon what the motorist says, if anything, and how the police officer responds.

For instance, in a police station in Norwich when no official breath-sampling device was available, a police officer asked a motorist if there were any reasons why a specimen of blood could not or should not be taken from him, and he replied, 'Yes, I am a diabetic and need two injections a day. I haven't been to a diabetic clinic for five years because I don't want other people putting needles in my arms and skin.'

The officer, noticing that the motorist had pierced ears and tattoos, did not think much of that answer and promptly asked him to supply a specimen of blood. The man, in effect, refused and was charged with failing to provide, without reasonable excuse, a specimen of his blood, contrary to Section 7 (6) of the 1988 Act.

The Norfolk stipendiary magistrate threw out the case and, when the Crown Prosecution Service appealed, his decision was upheld by the High Court. Mr Justice Butterfield said that, on hearing the driver's reply about his being a diabetic, etc., 'the constable should not have proceeded to require blood. The defendant had raised an objection based on his medical condition which, on its face, was not particularly convincing but should have caused the constable to delay making his request for blood until the police surgeon had expressed an opinion.'

And the judge laid down a proposition which is of general application in all such cases: 'The defendant was advancing reasons connected with his medical condition why he should not give a specimen of blood in response to the constable's warning. They may have been unconvincing reasons but it was not for the constable to substitute his opinion for that of a medical practitioner unless, of course, the reasons were so obviously frivolous that that could not, in any circumstances, amount to a medical condition providing significant reasons for refusing to provide a specimen.'

What it boils down to is that police officers should not be too cynical or disbelieving when a motorist says he does not want, for medical reasons, to give blood. But a further practical question arises: what is the legal position, if the police officer respects the motorist's objection and calls the police doctor – who then does not accept it and says that the blood test can proceed?

That is exactly what happened to Nigel Dempster, the well-known gossip columnist, who in April 1998 was convicted at West London Magistrates' Court of drink-driving, banned for a year, fined £250 and ordered to pay £300 costs. After inadvertently drinking alcohol when his daughter mixed orange juice in the fridge with vodka as a party prank, he gave a breath reading of 45 µg and, on being given the usual warning at a police station about the choice between blood and urine, said, 'I will give urine but under no circumstances will I give blood as I suffer from blood injury syndrome.' He explained that he had a life-long fear of needles since an incident as a twelve-year-old at boarding school when a doctor had made 'a tremendous mess' of his arm with a needle. He claimed that he had never been vaccinated and only once had had an injection.

Yet the police doctor, when called, said that in his opinion there were no clinical grounds for the objection. Whereupon, as laid down in the 1987 High Court case of *Rawlins* vs. *Brown*, Mr Dempster was convicted on the basis of the 45-µg reading which was, after all, 10 µg over the legal limit.

I am pleased to say that several months later his appeal against conviction was upheld and Judge Timothy Pontius said that the police doctor had been 'seriously wrong' in deciding that the defendant did not have a phobia about needles and blood. He awarded Mr Dempster his costs at both the lower and Appeal Courts. More importantly for motorists as a whole, he said that a lot of public time and money had been wasted and more consideration should be given to asking for urine tests as an alternative to blood tests.

I could not agree more. The notion of having to submit to blood being taken from your body against your will is both demeaning and barbaric. Many people do not like needles being pushed into their veins, even if this does not go as far as Nigel Dempster's phobia. If a motorist says, as Mr Dempster did, that he is happy to give urine, that should suffice. Drink-driving is a serious offence but human dignity also has its just demands.

How can you check the police reading of your blood or urine specimen?

The blood sample is divided between two containers, each labelled by the police doctor and countersigned by the police officer in charge. One container is then put into an envelope which is sealed and signed by both the doctor and police officer, and sent to a laboratory for testing. The police should offer you the other container for your own analysis. If they do not do this, you should still ask for it and have it analysed independently. Your solicitor will know how to find an expert analyst. With urine, the sample is also divided and put into two bottles. These are labelled and sealed with tape in your presence, and you will be asked to initial them. The police will send one bottle for their own analysis and should offer you the other for your own independent testing. Again, if it is not offered, ask for it and have it independently analysed.

If convicted, can you ever save your licence?

Only if you can persuade the magistrates that 'special reasons' exist. For instance, you only drove because of a sudden medical emergency and no other transportation was available; or someone had laced your drinks above the legal limit without your realizing it. But do not hope to argue that you were only just over the limit, or your driving was not impaired, or your livelihood would suffer, or you were drinking only a small amount on an empty stomach. You should have thought of that before having a drink.

*

And as if all this legal weaponry was not sufficiently intimidating, some police forces operate a policy of seizing drink-drivers' cars and upon conviction asking the magistrates to allow them to confiscate and sell the vehicles to promote road safety initiatives. This general power exists whenever anyone uses a vehicle in the commission of a crime, so why not apply it to the crime of drink-driving? The logic is unassailable.

BREATH TEST PROBLEMS

In recent years, two main problems have arisen, both of which have been overcome.

How does a motorist know the breathalyser is working properly?

A driver was stopped by police at 11.45 one morning. Her driving had not been erratic, she was not unsteady on her feet and her eyes were not glazed, but once she was stopped, the police noticed that her breath smelt of alcohol and asked her to take a roadside breath test. So far, so unquestionably legal. As I have written many times over the years, no one should think that random breath tests are unlawful. They are not! Section 163 of the 1988 Road Traffic Act states that a uniformed police officer can stop a motorist at any time when driving and ask to see his licence. And as far back as 1972 Lord Widgery, then Lord Chief Justice, ruled that if the officer then smells alcohol on the driver's breath, he can breath-test the motorist even though the driving had not been erratic and no moving traffic offence committed. As Lord Widgery said, 'The mere fact that a check can be described as random is no grounds for dismissing a drink-driving charge.'

However, what made this case exceptional was that this driver failed her breath test – and the subsequent Lion intoximeter reading of her breath at a police station revealed that she was four times over the limit!

But the Birmingham magistrates still dismissed a drink-driving charge on the basis that she had not consumed any alcohol since 11.30 the previous night (when, she claimed, she had drunk two cans of lager and a quarter of a bottle of whisky) and that, because of the long lapse of time, the lack of observable signs of intoxication, her rational, co-operative behaviour and the absence of any previous convictions, the intoximeter must have been unreliable and its reading was to be ignored. And they came to this conclusion despite the fact that there had been no expert or technical evidence to rebut a presumption imposed by the 1988 Act that an intoximeter, in use in a police station, is working properly.

The case was so important that the Director of Public Prosecutions appealed to the High Court in London where the acquittal was upheld – but not before two judges had scathing things to say about the magistrates' decision. Mr Justice Newman said that it 'was not one that no reasonable Bench could have made' and, therefore, in accordance with standard practice on appeals, it would have to be respected. But in future, he warned, any defendant wishing to make the point that a breath-testing device was unreliable should warn the prosecution beforehand so that they could call an expert to give evidence on the matter and if, without any such warning, the defence of unreliability was raised at trial, magistrates 'should respond favourably' to a prosecution application for an adjournment to call an expert to reply to it, and order the defendant to pay the costs of the adjournment.

Lord Justice Simon Brown went even further and said that the Birmingham magistrates' decision 'was very close to the line of perversity'.

When is a breath test 'oppressive' and therefore unlawful?

In Scotland, where drink-driving laws are the same as south of the Border, local police were running a pre-Christmas campaign to raise awareness of the 'morning after' effect. Accordingly, they were stopping all cars, telling drivers about the campaign and inviting them to take a roadside breath test. If they refused the test, they were allowed to proceed – unless, as in the English case of the Birmingham lady, the police smelt alcohol on a driver's breath, in which case they would be breath-tested.

This happened to one particular driver who failed both the roadside test and the subsequent intoximeter reading and was duly convicted. He appealed to the High Court of Justiciary in Edinburgh on the basis that the police action had been 'oppressive', a legitimate, if somewhat difficult to prove, ground of objection.

And so it was in this case. Lord Prosser said that the

only limit on police power to stop motorists contained in Section 163 of the 1988 Act was that it should not be exercised 'capriciously or oppressively'. This specific instance was part of 'a perfectly proper campaign' and the fact that the campaign was general ruled out oppression in the sense of unfair use of power against any particular citizen. The mere fact that a driver with alcohol on his breath had no choice, even though his driving could not be faulted, did not make his breath-testing 'oppressive' or unlawful.

The moral of these two cases from both sides of the Border is clear: the old days when our superior courts seemed sometimes all too ready to find reasons to quash drink-driving convictions have long gone.

BREATHLESS

If you genuinely cannot provide the breath for a breath test, what is the next step? What can the police do?

It depends on what stage has been reached. If you have just been stopped and are being breathalysed at the roadside to establish whether you should be arrested and taken to a police station for a full computer print-out test of your blood alcohol content, and you are unable to provide breath, the police officer can still arrest you and carry on the process. It does not matter whether your inability to give a breath sample is genuine. You will still see the inside of a police station.

But if the officer thinks you are not genuine, the situation is even worse. Section 6 (4) of the 1988 Road Traffic Act makes it a specific offence to fail 'without reasonable excuse' to provide a roadside breath sample. You will not necessarily be banned. But you may be fined up to £1,000, your licence will be endorsed and you will get four penalty points as well as incurring any drink-driving penalty.

But if you 'cannot' supply a breath specimen at a police station, the consequences are even more serious. If the police believe there is a medical reason for this, they can ask you to supply blood or urine instead. If they believe you are faking, they can call off the drink-driving procedure and charge you with failing 'without reasonable excuse' to provide a police station breath specimen, contrary to Section 7 (6) of the 1988 Act.

Now you are really in trouble. You can be jailed for up to six months or fined up to £5,000, or both, you will certainly be banned from driving (often for longer than if you had been guilty only of drink-driving), and your licence will be endorsed with three to eleven penalty points.

But one important legal question remains: if you genuinely cannot provide a breath specimen, whether the roadside or police station version, can you avoid a failing-to-provide conviction by alleging 'reasonable excuse'? Usually the answer is 'No' – unless you have strong medical evidence in support or (even more rarely) you can satisfy the Bench that you were suffering from such shock or stress that you were physically unable to comply with the police's request.

In 1972 Lord Justice Lawton laid down sternly: 'No excuse can be adjudged reasonable unless [the motorist] is physically or mentally unable to provide it or the provision of the specimen would entail a substantial risk to his health.' But in 1987 Mr Justice Pain commented in the High Court that he would have been 'sorry to see a man who had really tried ... none the less be convicted'. That view no longer prevails. In January 1990 Lord Justice Watkins said the comment should be disregarded: 'I believe it contrary to a broad spectrum of authority.' In a case where Hampshire magistrates had thrown out a failing-to-provide charge against a thirty-five-year-old physically fit driver who had drunk six pints and then failed to provide a breath specimen, although insisting 'he had tried his best', Lord Justice Watkins said, 'Justices must be very careful not to be so gullible.'

But Lord Justice Lloyd has since softened the official line. It was in a case where a driver had given one breath specimen at the station but lost composure when asked for a second. She blew into the device but could not find sufficient breath. She was sobbing continuously and clearly distraught. Magistrates threw out a failing-to-provide charge because she had 'a reasonable excuse'. The prosecution appealed to the High Court – and lost. Lord Justice Lloyd said, 'The fact that a defendant is drunk or under stress is not of itself sufficient to provide him with a reasonable excuse. Nor is it sufficient that he was doing his best or trying his hardest, otherwise the purpose of the Act would be defeated. But here the facts go further. This defendant's state of shock was a substantial factor in her inability to provide a specimen. The justices heard her give evidence. They were clearly impressed. It would not be right for this court to interfere.'

Judicial tolerance of human frailty exists. But it is not to be taken for granted – or abused.

BUYING A NEW CAR

For most people, buying a new car is their biggest single investment after buying their home. You will almost certainly be buying from a dealer and you have certain basic protection under the 1979 Sale of Goods Act, as amended by the 1994 Sale and Supply of Goods Act. Under these two Acts, a dealer must ensure that the car is reasonably fit for the purpose for which it was bought (i.e. to be driven!), is of 'satisfactory quality' and conforms to any description he has given you, and that he has the right to sell it.

Dealers are usually franchised by the manufacturer, and there are generally manufacturers' warranties that add to your legal rights but cannot replace or curtail them (see **Extended Warranties**). If a newly bought car does not perform well, you should promptly contact the dealer and put your complaint in writing; do not be tempted to have the car repaired, although if you do, you may still be able to return it and claim your money back; do not drive it again hoping that the fault will 'sort itself out', and, above all, return the car and demand a replacement vehicle. Your contract is with the dealer, so do not be fobbed off by being told to contact the manufacturer.

(See also **Registering Your Car.**)

C

CARAVANS

There are two main aspects of the law in relation to driving with a caravan.

Towing

Legally caravans are merely a special kind of trailer and you will need to fit exterior towing mirrors on your car so that you have a clear view along both sides of the car and the caravan. You must, when practicable, pull over if you are holding up a stream of traffic (see **Holiday Driving in the UK**). You must not let anyone ride in the caravan when it is being towed and you cannot tow a caravan or any other kind of trailer in the outside lane of a motorway which has more than two lanes, unless other lanes are closed. The National Caravan Council (see **Useful Addresses**) publishes an informative booklet, *The Caravan Towing Guide*, which covers all aspects of the subject.

Speed limits

Outside built-up areas, motor vehicles towing a caravan or trailer cannot exceed 60 mph on a motorway or dual carriageway, or 50 mph on a single carriageway, unless traffic signs indicate otherwise.

Caravan sites

These cannot be established without planning permission and a site licence. Once permission has been granted, the local authority must issue a licence specifying what type of site is allowed and how it will be run. The licence may restrict the number of caravans that can be parked and control their positions so that, for example, they will not be clearly visible from outside the site. The licence will also cover public health matters, such as fire precautions and the provision of adequate sanitary facilities. In order to enforce the licence conditions, the local authority can inspect the site and, as a last resort, has the right to take away the licence. As for parking caravans on common land, this is usually prohibited, although some local by-laws allow it. It is always worthwhile checking beforehand with the National Caravanning Council.

CARELESS DRIVING

We have all been guilty of this at some time, although most of us have never been caught, but what exactly is the offence of careless driving?

Section 3 of the 1988 Road Traffic Act creates two possible offences: (1) driving a motor vehicle on a road or other public place without due care and attention or (2) without reasonable consideration for other persons using the road or place.

The penalties are the same: a maximum fine of £2,500

(although usually very much lower sums are imposed), endorsement with three to nine penalty points and very rare disqualification.

The Crown Prosecution Service has to be careful which version of the offence to bring as a charge. Driving at night on a busy road with headlamps on main beam – potentially blinding oncoming traffic – may or may not amount to driving 'without due care and attention' and an astute defence lawyer might secure an acquittal. But a charge of driving 'without reasonable consideration for other road users' would almost certainly succeed.

A driver can be convicted of driving without reasonable consideration for his own passenger. That was Lord Chief Justice Lord Parker's ruling in May 1965 when the driver of a double-decker bus was prosecuted after five passengers had complained about his taking several sharp bends at high speed.

But what exactly does the law mean by 'careless'? I can do no better than quote the latest (2000) edition of *Stone's Justices' Manual*: 'In order to secure a conviction for driving without due care and attention, the prosecutor must prove beyond a reasonable doubt that the defendant was not exercising that degree of care and attention that a reasonable and prudent driver would exercise in the circumstances. *That standard is an objective one, impersonal and universal, fixed in relation to the safety of other users of the highway.*'

The words I have italicized mean that there are precious few excuses for a charge of careless driving that a court will accept. It is no defence that a learner or inexperienced driver or someone tired after a long journey was doing their genuine best, if that best falls short of the standard to be expected from a reasonably competent driver. All cases are judged on their own facts and magistrates take all the circumstances into account. Failing to observe the Highway Code does not automatically ensure a conviction but is almost impossible to get round.

The truth is that the most minor error of judgement can technically amount to careless driving. Whether you get charged depends on how tolerant the local police force is, and whether you get convicted on how liberal the local magistrates are.

Driving too slowly when looking for a place to park, signalling left then turning right, not slowing down to avoid splashing pedestrians, changing your mind about which side road to turn into, turning to the right from the inside lane at a T-junction or waiting until the last moment before you indicate: all of these could, if challenged in the courts, result in careless driving convictions – whether or not they result in an accident.

Just as there does not have to be an accident for a charge of careless driving to succeed, you cannot say that because there has been an accident, someone must have been driving so carelessly as to involve the law. As the late Sir Ernest Milton, when Chief Metropolitan Magistrate at London's Bow Street Court, once lamented: 'Is it necessary every time there is a bump for everyone to come rushing along here? There is no need to bring every careless motorist to a magistrates' court.' As a Justice of the Peace friend told me, 'If every motorist guilty of careless driving were to be brought before the courts, we would have little time for anything else.' In today's overcrowded and inadequate roads, careless driving is a fact of everyday motoring life.

CAR PARKS

Can you be guilty of drink-driving if the police stop you in a pub car park just before you actually drive out on to the road? Can a shopper who has to jump hurriedly out of your way complain to the police that you have been guilty of careless driving because while making a beeline for an empty space you ignored traffic-flow arrows in a supermarket car park?

These are not just academic posers. Little-known provisions of the 1991 Road Traffic Act that came into effect in July 1992 have brought car parks into the forefront of motoring law.

Until July 1992, only two offences (drink-driving, when a motorist has excess alcohol in his system, and drunken driving, where he is 'unfit to drive through drink') could be committed in a car park: the 1988 Road Traffic Act states that these offences were punishable if committed 'on a road or other public place'. And it was well-established judge-made law that a car park could be 'a public place' if the public were entitled to park their cars there or were invited or permitted to do so, or if the vehicles' presence was tolerated or merely probable (even when the car park was officially closed), *but* only so long as the drivers whose cars were parked in the car park had not 'ceased to be members of the general public and become instead a special class', as Lord Justice Simon Brown said in March 1991.

In that case, a caravan was parked on privately owned land to which entry could only be obtained by paying a small registration fee and obtaining a car pass. Magistrates threw out a drink-driving charge against a motorist with a pass who was involved in an accident in the car park because they ruled it was not 'a public place'. But the High Court sent the case back to them with a direction to convict. As Lord Justice Brown laid down, 'A mere fondness for camping and caravanning cannot constitute a peculiarity sufficient to distinguish those who display [the pass] from their fellow citizens. Up to the boundary of this caravan site those seeking entry are unarguably members of the general public pure and simple. It is quite unreal to suggest that at the gate some transformation occurs whereby they alter their legal character, shed their identity as members of the general public and take on a different status as caravanners and campers.'

The significance of this ruling is that it is now much easier to argue successfully that a car park is a 'public place'. Because the 1991 Road Traffic Act says that dangerous and careless driving can be committed in a 'public place' as well as on a road, the result is that most car parks, including supermarket and multi-storey parks, have ceased to be a legal no man's land for bad drivers.

Nowadays, in nearly all car parks, if you ignore direction arrows, no-entry signs or speed limits or are otherwise guilty of careless or dangerous driving, you run the risk of a magistrates' court summons if someone reports you to the police.

But even without bringing in the criminal law, motorists cannot treat car parks as if they were a legal no man's land. If, for instance, you crash into an unattended parked car and you know it was your fault, you should leave a note of your name and address on the windscreen – but how many people are that honest?

CAR SHARING

Greater car sharing forms an important part of John Prescott's controversial, if ill-defined, integrated transport policy. This prompts me to consider: what is your legal liability to your passenger? The question may seem simple but there are perhaps some surprises in the answer.

For a start, you cannot contract out of your liability. You cannot, in effect, say to your passenger, 'You are driving with me at your own risk. I am not accepting any responsibility – nor is my insurance company – if we have an accident.' The reason is that Section 149 of the 1988 Road Traffic Act specifies that no 'agreement or understanding' between the driver and passenger of a motor vehicle can stop the passenger suing if injured through the driver's negligence.

Yet compulsory insurance for liability to passengers is a

comparatively recent development. It was only the 1972 Road Traffic Act that first extended the notion of compulsory third-party cover against death or bodily injury to include a passenger as a 'third party'. And it was not until the 1988 Road Traffic Act that cover was extended to a passenger's property.

Similarly, until 1978 it used to be unlawful for a motorist – driving to work with colleagues, for instance – to share the cost of travel with passengers. But nowadays non-profit car sharing is allowed, if (depending on the size of the vehicle) no more than eight people are travelling and any charges for petrol, oil, etc. are agreed before the journey starts.

Your insurance cover will not be affected. But, of course, an insurance company will usually only pay out if there is legal liability anyway, and that means your driving must have been at fault. 'Negligence' in civil law is much the same as 'driving without due care and attention' in criminal law.

Family or social relationships are irrelevant. A husband can find himself suing his wife, a daughter her father, a boyfriend his girlfriend and vice versa: it depends on who was driving. In one tragic case, a woman teacher who suffered 'appalling injuries' when being driven by her brother on a holiday in Scotland was awarded £225,000 agreed damages against him in the High Court; but, of course, it was his insurance company that actually paid out.

There is an interesting legal quirk if a passenger is injured when two cars collide. It will then be easier and quicker to sue only one's own driver, leaving it to him to bring in the other motorist as co-defendant. Often the passenger will then drop out of the courtroom battle altogether. Why? Because if the passenger's own driver is only as little as 1 per cent to blame, that will still suffice to make him liable for *all* the passenger's damages.

So insurance companies generally cut their costs by paying the passenger's claim in full, leaving the real dispute as to apportionment of liability to be fought out between the two drivers. The passenger usually gets his money long before either driver!

But there is one important limitation on passengers' rights. The law recognizes that, just as a driver can be guilty of negligence, so a passenger can be guilty of 'contributory negligence' in not taking reasonable care for his own safety. That is why injured adult passengers who do not use their seat-belts and unthinking individuals who go out on a motorized 'pub crawl' with a driver friend who they know will probably drink too much will both have their damages reduced.

Not only drivers must remember that a car is a lethal weapon. So must their passengers.

CHILDREN

Modern criminal law is extremely complex. For instance, when my son was a baby, I used to put him in a carry-cot on the rear seat of the car, but if a police officer were to see me doing a similar thing today, I would almost certainly receive a fixed-penalty notice or be fined. Nowadays the use of a carry-cot, on either a front or a rear seat, is permitted *but only if the cot is strapped*. You must put the seat-belt around it and fasten it. Otherwise you could be in trouble!

It is illegal nowadays to carry any unrestrained child in the front seat of a car. A child under three can only travel legally in a front seat if an appropriate child restraint is worn. ('Appropriate child restraint' means a baby carrier, child seat, harness or booster seat appropriate to the child's weight, which will be clearly marked on the label.) The DETR advises that if no child restraint is available for a child under three, it is generally safer for it to wear an adult seat-belt alone, in the rear seat, than no restraint at all.

Between the ages of three and eleven, a 'small child' (i.e. under 1.5 metres, about 5 feet, tall) can travel in the front seat with a child restraint, if available. If there is no child restraint in the front or rear, however, but an adult seat-belt is fitted in front, that is where the child must travel. The child *can* travel in the rear but a child restraint or adult seat-belt must be worn, if available.

A child aged twelve or thirteen or a 'large child' (i.e. 1.5 metres, about 5 feet, or taller) under that age can sit in the front or the back of a car – but an adult seat-belt must be worn, if available.

With a child of fourteen or over, adult seat-belt rules apply (see **Seat-belts**).

I said that the subject was complex!

COMPANY CARS

These are the ultimate status symbol of middle management, and have obvious advantages. Running your own car may well be cheaper because employees pay income tax at 35 per cent on a company car's purchase price (subject to reduction according to the car's age, the employee's earnings and the number of business miles), but having a company car remains a major fringe benefit for most workers. In fact, the loss of a company car figures in many claims for compensation for unfair dismissal.

The precise value of the benefit will depend on the terms that you can negotiate with your employer. You may be able to obtain the right to top up his contribution so that you can buy a car outside the price range available. In those circumstances, the car will usually still be the company's, not yours – but it will make much more of an impression on the neighbours!

Furthermore, at the very least, you should ensure that the company will pay for taxing, insuring and servicing the car as well as for all petrol used on business trips. If they appreciate your services sufficiently, some employers can even be persuaded to pay for petrol for private as well as business use, although you then may have to pay tax on that element of free petrol.

The important thing to remember is that ownership of the car – yours or the boss's – does not affect the question of liability in the event of an accident. If you are at fault in the course of what was purely a private trip, you alone will be responsible for paying compensation – even if you were driving a company car. Irrespective of legal ownership, a company is only liable for the negligent driving of its employee if he was driving within the course of his employment.

COURT CASES

Having defended many motorists in court, I can only report that you should, as a general rule, plead guilty and not fight a driving case unless (a) you have a burning sense of injustice (sadly, not always an infallible guide to courtroom success), (b) a competent lawyer advises that you have a good defence in law, and (c), either way, you can afford it – going to court does not come cheap.

It is not enough to say, 'I shall tell the truth on oath. They must believe me!' It does not always work out like that. Some years ago, a bishop contested a speeding summons and was astonished that the Bench accepted a policeman's word, 'corroborated' by what he said was the reading on his motorcycle's speedometer, against his own testimony in the witness box. 'I am staggered that they accepted the policeman's evidence and not mine,' he afterwards told a reporter. He even threatened to resign.

With motoring cases, you never can tell. I have won cases that I thought I would lose and lost others that I thought I had a reasonable chance of winning. It is almost – but not quite – a lottery.

Most motoring offences not dealt with by the fixed penalty system can be dealt with by post and, if you plead guilty, a short, courteous letter expressing your regret, stating such mitigation as may be available, and apologizing to the court, can do no harm. Otherwise, even if pleading guilty, you may sometimes still have to go to court to give an account of your side of things. This applies if the court is considering the possibility of disqualification (*of which it must notify you in advance*) or if you want to argue that 'special reasons' exist mitigating against endorsement of your licence. Then, if you can possibly afford it, you should engage a lawyer to speak for you and, if necessary, take you through your story in the witness box.

How do you find a solicitor, whether to represent you on a plea of guilty or to contest the case, if you really are determined to challenge the police evidence and go for an outright acquittal? Many people have to rely upon the free legal representation provided by their motoring organization, whether the AA or the RAC, or take up personal recommendations from friends. But the Law Society, the professional body that represents the 80,000 solicitors in England and Wales, launched in September 2000 a brand-new website, *www.solicitors-online.com*, which now offers contact details of all its members throughout the country. Visitors to the site can find details of solicitors in their area who specialize in the type of legal service they require. As Michael Napier, President of the Law Society, said at the time of the launch: 'This site should make it simpler than ever to find a solicitor to help with your legal needs.' In the rare case when you will need a barrister to represent you (usually because the case has legal complications or because you need a strong and skilful cross-examiner), you must first go through a solicitor who will generally have an unofficial 'panel' of the barristers that he uses.

And you should always ask your solicitor to find an experienced *local* barrister who, if it is a criminal matter, knows that particular Bench of magistrates well and often appears in front of them, or likewise the circuit judge in the local County Court, if it is a civil matter, such as making or defending a claim for damages after an accident. This also applies if the solicitor is not handling the case himself but using a local solicitor acting as his agent. Personal experience of the magistrates or judge – their idiosyncracies, their policy with regard to specific matters, even their ill-disguised prejudices – is always immensely useful.

D

DANGEROUS DRIVING

How 'dangerous' does dangerous driving have to be?
What is the difference between dangerous and careless
driving? Do you really know?

The difference in penalty is certainly substantial: dangerous driving carries up to two years' imprisonment and/or
an unlimited fine, with obligatory disqualification for at
least one year and endorsement with three to eleven penalty points, if no 'special reasons' exist. Careless driving
attracts no possibility of prison but, without 'special reason', a maximum £2,500 fine, with discretionary disqualification for a short period, only a few months at the most,
plus endorsement with three to nine penalty points.

Yet the police and the courts somehow have difficulty
in deciding just how bad the quality of the driving must
be to qualify as merely careless as opposed to dangerous.

Parliament has not helped all that much. Section 2A of
the 1988 Road Traffic Act states: 'A person is to be
regarded as driving dangerously if, and only if, (a) the way
he drives falls far below [this vague phrase is nowhere
defined] what would be expected of a competent and
careful driver and (b) it would be obvious to a competent
and careful driver that driving in that way would be

dangerous.' In other words, dangerous means dangerous. Big deal.

As for careless driving, Section 3 of the 1988 Road Traffic Act creates two versions of the same offence: driving 'without due care and attention' and driving 'without reasonable consideration for other persons' (see **Careless Driving**). Again, there is no further definition. The result of this sloppy parliamentary draftsmanship is that the ordinary motorist – not to mention the police and even some magistrates – can easily be unsure about what exactly the difference is between dangerous and careless driving, other than the vague notion that the one is more serious than the other.

Fortunately, in March 1996 the Crown Prosecution Service published valuable new official guidance 'to help police and prosecutors make the right choice when there is more than one charge available following a driving incident'. It has undoubtedly helped the authorities but it also deserves to be better known by the motoring public generally.

For its strength lies in its concrete examples, as well as its statement of the law. Hence: careless driving is stated to be acts of driving caused by more than momentary inattention in which road users' safety is affected, such as overtaking on the inside, driving inappropriately close to another vehicle or driving through a red light. Also stigmatized as careless driving is conduct that clearly caused the driver not to be in a position to respond in the event of an emergency, such as using a hand-held mobile telephone while the vehicle is moving (especially when at speed), tuning a car radio, or reading a newspaper or map.

Driving without reasonable consideration is instanced as: flashing lights to force other drivers in front to give way, misuse of any lane to avoid queueing or gain some other advantage over other drivers, unnecessarily remaining in an overtaking lane, driving unnecessarily slowly or braking without good cause.

What about dangerous driving? Examples are given as: racing or competitive driving; highly inappropriate speed for prevailing road or traffic conditions; aggressive or intimidatory driving, such as sudden lane changes, cutting into a line of vehicles or driving too close to the vehicle in front, especially when the purpose is to cause the other vehicle to pull to one side to allow the accused to overtake; deliberate disregard of traffic lights or other road signs; and prolonged, persistent or deliberate bad driving.

So now we have positive guidelines on the precise legal status of various kinds of bad driving that we see far too often. But why was this not available for earlier generations of motorists?

DEATH ON THE ROADS

Even the best driver can find himself in the dire plight of causing death on the road. With thousands of people killed every year on our roads, this is sadly a question of practical interest to everyone who drives.

The penalty, if any, depends upon the specific motoring offence committed. Victims' sorrowing relatives may not agree but judges are continually saying, and most motorists would say rightly, that you cannot argue backwards from the consequences of a particular piece of driving and say, 'Somebody was killed. So the level of bad driving must necessarily have been the worst.'

Any experienced motoring lawyer knows that a person can be killed on the roads without a driver being legally – or even morally – to blame. Some accidents just happen while others are quite honestly the victim's own fault. And even if a motorist is to blame, it may be merely momentary inattention or an untypical error of judgement by someone with a good driving record.

So what are the major offences with which a driver involved in a fatal accident on a road – or other public place – may be faced?

Manslaughter

This is the most serious – but also the rarest. It carries a maximum penalty of life imprisonment and is usually reserved for joyriding adults who drive with no concern for their own or anyone else's safety. This form of manslaughter, where the prosecution has to prove not merely dangerous or careless driving but 'gross negligence' is difficult to prove. Acquittals are quite frequent, as in a case at Nottingham Crown Court in August 2000 where a Royal Navy pilot who had crashed his car, killing one of three passengers, while on a late-night joyride around Silverstone race circuit was acquitted after a trial lasting two and a half days. The car overturned on a bend after time spent in a hospitality tent but the jury accepted that the thirty-

three-year-old driver, who admitted drinking six pints of
lager, had been guilty of misjudgement – but not of gross
negligence. It will be noted that this tragic accident
occurred in a public place – i.e. a race circuit – not on a
road; but, if proved, the offence would still have been
committed. The location would have made no difference to
the final result.

Causing death by careless driving while under the influence of drink or drugs or with excess alcohol in the body

Section 3A of the 1991 Road Traffic Act created this offence
with a penalty of disqualification (and a new 'extended'
driving test) except for 'special reasons' and a maximum
five years in prison, quickly increased to ten years by the
1993 Criminal Justice Act. Appeal Court decisions have
since indicated that the *average* sentence should be around
the old maximum of five years.

But a drink-driving conviction is not essential to obtain
a satisfactory result. The Act also makes it an offence if
within eighteen hours of the accident the motorist, without
reasonable excuse, fails to give a breath specimen if asked
to do so by the police. In August 2000, a twenty-four-year-
old driver who four years before had fatally injured his
unborn son when he had driven his car too fast on a foggy
night and had veered off a country lane and ploughed into
a ditch was jailed for seven years at Leicester Crown Court.
He was driving his pregnant girlfriend and had not given
a breath specimen within eighteen hours of the accident,
so, even though there was no conviction for drink-driving

to help the jury, they were still able to find him guilty of an offence against Section 3A.

Causing death through dangerous driving

Section 1 of the 1991 Act created this other new offence with disqualification (and a new 'extended' driving test) in the absence of 'special reasons' and a maximum five years in prison, again increased to ten years by the 1993 Act. This is the offence with which a normally careful motorist with a good driving record is most likely to be charged.

Sentences vary from six months to four years, depending on the circumstances. For instance, a fifty-four-year-old retired millionaire businessman who killed two pensioners when he crashed into their car while showing off his wife's £130,000 Ferrari at high speed, was jailed for nine months. He was banned from driving for seven years and Judge David Wilcox told him at Shrewsbury Crown Court that the public would have been 'outraged' if he had not sent him to jail, even though he had suffered severe depression since the crash.

At the lowest level of culpability, a motorist can be charged merely with careless driving, carrying only a maximum fine of £2,500 with no risk of jail and only discretionary disqualification (i.e. even without 'special reasons'). I will deal with these cases later under **Killing While Careless**.

One final thought. I am not sure that everyone will agree, but I ask you to consider these words of the late Lord Taylor, then Lord Chief Justice, in December 1993:

'We wish to stress that human life cannot be restored nor even its loss measured by the length of a prison sentence. We recognize that no term of months or years imposed on the offender can reconcile the family of a deceased victim to their loss nor will it cure their anguish.'

Or lessen the long-lasting sense of guilt of any decent motorist.

DOUBLE WHITE LINES

Even the least experienced driver knows that double white lines in the middle of the road mean that you cannot cross them, even to overtake an appallingly slow-moving vehicle. You must simply be patient. You can only escape conviction for crossing these double lines if you can persuade a court that you needed to do so, in order, for instance, to turn into a side road or on to land adjoining the highway; to pass a stationary vehicle; to avoid an accident; to pass someone riding a bicycle or horse at less than 10 miles an hour – or owing to circumstances outside your control.[1] Notice that reference to 'a stationary vehicle'. Most motorists would have assumed that it should not have been there anyway: that, in fact, double white lines mean 'no stopping' as well as 'no overtaking'.

---

1 One might wonder why, if you can overtake a really slow cyclist or horse rider, you cannot overtake other really slow vehicles, such as farm vehicles. The simple answer is that Regulation 26 of the 1994 Traffic Signs Regulations does not mention them!

But what about stopping for the limited purpose of picking up or setting down passengers? Is that allowed or does it come within the general prohibition on all stopping?

The Highway Code seems to have no doubt that this limited form of stopping is lawful. Rule 215 states clearly: 'You MUST NOT stop or park on a road marked with double white lines, except to pick up or set down passengers.' Yet two separate courts, the magistrates' court at Bishops Stortford and, on appeal, the St Albans Crown Court, ruled, on a strict interpretation of Regulation 26 of the 1994 Traffic Signs Regulations and General Directions, that picking up or setting down passengers is a legal excuse only if it has to be done on that particular section of road and cannot be done anywhere else along that road where there are no central double white lines.

They therefore convicted a taxi driver of breaching Regulation 26, because he could have picked up or set down his passenger further down the road. So what happened? He appealed to the High Court, where Lord Justice Pill and Mr Justice Newman quashed the conviction and ruled, in a decision which applies to all motorists, that a vehicle can lawfully stop 'for as long as necessary to enable a person to board or alight'. There is no obligation to move on further down the road – even if there are double white lines in the middle of the road.

But I would still warn: the very existence of the double white lines necessarily limits the amount of road area available to motorists in any one direction. So a prudent motorist should take care to ensure that, by choosing to stop, he is not thereby creating a potential hazard for others.

DRIVER

This seems a simple enough word, but few things are simple in the law and this is no exception.The 1988 Road Traffic Act, which is the most important of all the statutes dealing with motoring law, contemplates that there can be more than one 'driver' of a vehicle at the same time. Hence, Section 192 (1) gives this general, not particularly helpful, definition: 'Where a separate person acts as steersman of a motor vehicle, "driver" includes that person as well as any other person engaged in the driving of the vehicle.'

As the High Court ruled in *R.* v. *MacDonagh* in 1974, the essence of driving is the use of the driver's controls in order to direct movement, however that movement is obtained. Accordingly, a person who sits in the driver's seat of a vehicle and controls it while it is being towed is driving the vehicle (*McQuaid* v. *Anderton* in 1980), and so is a person sitting in the driver's seat and setting the car in motion, even though he has no keys, the engine is not running and the steering is locked (*Burgoyne* v. *Phillips* in 1982). It has even been held in 1976 in *Tyler* v. *Whatmore*, a case brought under the Motor Vehicles (Construction and Use) Regulations, that a woman was one of the two 'drivers' while she was in the passenger seat, leaning across and controlling the steering-wheel, handbrake and ignition while her male companion in the driving seat operated the gears and foot controls. But a front-seat passenger who momentarily grabs the steering-wheel cannot properly be said to be driving the car: in borderline cases it is important to consider the length of time the steering-wheel or other control was handled (*Jones* v. *Pratt* in 1983). The steersman of a towed vehicle is undoubtedly driving it for the purpose of the offence of driving while disqualified. Similarly, if the vehicle is being pushed, a person at the wheel would be in the category of driver.

Nice distinctions are continually being made. Hence, a person walking beside a vehicle which is being pushed or moving under gravity will not be 'driving' merely because he has his hand on the steering-wheel (*R.* v. *MacDonagh* in 1974). But, in the case of a motorcycle, it has been held that a person who sits astride it and propels it with his feet in a paddling movement, with hands on the handlebars so as to control direction, but without the engine running, is 'driving' it (*Gunnell* v. *DPP* in 1994).

NOTE: I am grateful to the latest (2000) edition of *Stone's Justices' Manual* for the uniquely authoritative basis of this summary.

DRIVING LICENCE

This is, of course, an essential document and to obtain it you must first pass a driving test (see following entry). Your examiner will issue you with a form which you must

fill in and send to the DVLA, an Executive Agency of the
DETR, together with the appropriate fee and your driving-
test pass certificate that he will give you. As from July 1997
the DVLA only issues photocard-style driving licences, and
they require a passport photograph, together with a signed
declaration from 'someone of standing', e.g. a magistrate,
doctor, barrister, minister of religion. You will also have to
supply your passport or birth certificate.

On receipt, you must promptly sign your full licence –
it is technically an offence not to do so. The licence will
only entitle you to drive the type of vehicle with which
you have passed the test. If you have passed with an
automatic car, you will not be allowed to drive a manual
one. However, passing on a manual will allow you to drive
an automatic.

A full licence usually lasts until you are seventy, after
which you can go on renewing it for three years at a time
at a cost (at the time of writing) of £8.50. A photocard
licence has to be renewed every ten years until you are
seventy, in order to keep your photograph up to date.

There are only two ways to lose your licence against
your will. The first is if a court disqualifies you from
driving. This will be for a fixed period which, depending
on the offence, can be for anything from several weeks or
months to, in theory, life – although I honestly do not
know of any such case. In practice, twenty years is the
longest likely disqualification – for a persistently bad driver
with a truly appalling record.

The second way to lose your licence is to develop a
major physical disability, such as epilepsy, 'likely', as the

1988 Road Traffic Act puts it, 'to make your driving a source of danger to the public'. You must then inform the DVLA which may, after a medical examination, revoke your licence. But you can appeal to a magistrates' court.

Section 163 of the 1988 Act gives a uniformed police officer the right to stop you at any time, for any reason whatseover, when you are driving and Section 164 gives him the right to do so for the specific purpose of seeing your licence. If you do not produce it then or at a police station of your choice within seven days or 'as soon as reasonably practicable' thereafter, you commit an offence for which you can be fined up to £1,000. Driving without having a licence at all is, of course, much more serious. You can be fined up to £1,000, have three to six penalty points endorsed on any licence that you may obtain in future and even, in a really bad case, be disqualified.

DRIVING TEST

You cannot legally drive without passing the test and in recent years it has been made even more difficult. From May 1999 candidates are not considered competent to drive if they commit fifteen minor driving faults or one serious fault during their driving test. Today's test – unlike when I passed mine a long time ago – is in two parts: written and practical. Would-be drivers must pass the written test before being allowed to take the practical and, if they fail, they can retake it within three days; if they fail the practical, they have up to two years in which to retake and pass it. If not, they must start all over again with another written test. The pass rate at the first attempt is about 50 per cent. If you fail the practical test, you must wait one month before applying for another test. If you feel that the examiner did not conduct the test properly, you can appeal to a magistrates' court – but this is very rarely done and your prospects of success are virtually nil.

To take your test, you will have to complete a form available from post offices confirming that you pass the minimum legal eyesight test (i.e. you can read a number plate at 20.5 metres, or 67 feet, with or without spectacles). You will send this to the Clerk to the Traffic Commissioners for your area to arrange a date for an on-road driving test. If the examiner is then satisfied that you have sat and passed your written test and (since January 1997) completed your off-road Compulsory Basic Training (CBT) if you want to drive a moped or motorcycle, he will subject you to a practical driving test on ordinary roads and if you prove yourself, in his opinion, competent to drive, he will give you a driving-test pass certificate which will enable you to convert your provisional driving licence (see the following paragraph) into a full one. In the unlikely event of anyone not applying to the DVLA for their full licence within two years, the test is nullified and the whole process must be restarted. Furthermore, any new driver clocking up six or more penalty points within those first two years will also have to take the test again.

But, of course, before even applying for a driving test,

you must first learn to drive. The basic minimum requirements are that learners must be at least seventeen, hold a
provisional licence (obtainable for £21 at a post office),
display on the back and front of the vehicle L-plates of
a type specified in the 1999 Motor Vehicles (Driving
Licence) Regulations (a red letter 'L', 102 mm high by 89
mm wide by 38 mm thick, on a white card 178 mm
square), or, in Wales, D-plates (from the Welsh *dysgwr*,
meaning 'learner'), with similar measurements – and not
drive on motorways. The learner must also be accompanied by someone aged at least twenty-one who has held
a full British licence for that type of car for at least three
years.

But there is much more to it than that.

Professional instructors who teach learners for payment
must be approved by the DVLA, which keeps a register
of approved driving instructors who must display their
approval certificate in their tuition car. But even non-pro-
fessionals cannot simply sit back and enjoy the scenery.
They must supervise the driving of the novice at the
wheel.

If not, *both* the supervising and the learner driver can
find themselves in legal trouble. Back in 1940, in a case
where the supervising driver had failed to warn a learner
not to overtake before a dangerous bend and he had
crashed into an oncoming lorry, a High Court judge upheld
the learner's conviction of careless driving *and* his companion's conviction of aiding and abetting. Mr Justice
Hilbery ruled: 'It is the supervisor's duty, when necessary,
to do whatever can reasonably be expected to prevent the

driver from acting unskilfully or carelessly or in a manner likely to cause danger to others.'

That still remains the law – for all motoring offences. Technically, the supervising driver may even be guilty of aiding and abetting – and, therefore, also liable to be fined – when a learner commits a simple parking offence.

Similar considerations apply if the learner has an accident and the victim sues him for damages. As Lord Denning once said, 'It is no answer to say, "I was a learner driver under instructions. I was doing my best and could not help it." The law requires the same standard of care as from any other driver. He may be doing his best but his incompetent best is not good enough.'

This ruling has two by-products.

The learner – or his insurance company – may even have to pay damages to his own accompanying driver, if reasonable supervision could not have prevented the accident. But the supervisor would have to prove – *and this is most important* – that he had not accepted the risk of uncompensated injury by, for instance, checking beforehand with the learner that he was insured.

If, however, the accident could have been avoided by reasonable supervision (grabbing the wheel or handbrake, even just shouting), the so-called supervisor would have to share in any damages paid to an injured third party, and damages for his own injuries would be cut because of his own 'contributory negligence'.

There is one other vitally important point for learners – and for any qualified driver allowing a learner to drive his car. The driving will *not* be covered by insurance unless the car owner has previously told his insurance company. They must be given an opportunity to charge an increased premium because there is a learner at the wheel.

Many people do not always realize what they are taking on when helping a relative or friend to learn to drive.

(See also **Learner Drivers**.)

DRUGS

My colleague Andrew English, in an article entitled 'Unfit to Drive' in the *Daily Telegraph* of 2 October 1999, highlighted senior police officers' doubts about their ability to prove driving impairment when a rising number of drug-users are taking their cars on to our roads. According to Section 4 (5) of the 1988 Road Traffic Act, you cannot be guilty of driving a motor vehicle while unfit to drive through drink or drugs 'unless your ability to drive properly is for the time being impaired'. Yet, as Andrew wrote, 'knowing that a drug is in your system is not the same as proving that it is impairing your driving; and cannabis brings its own problems in this respect'.

Ironically, the very next week my copy of the latest (19th) edition of *Wilkinson's Road Traffic Offences*, the motoring lawyers' bible, arrived through the post, and at once I found a reference to the uniquely authoritative nineteen-month-old High Court decision in *Leetham* v. *DPP*, which goes a long way to help solve the problem. It is typical of the cack-handed way in which valuable cases are reported in this country that this decision, of immense practical importance, has not appeared in any of the normal Law Reports or in *Current Law*, the essential monthly digest of new cases and statutes, but in the highly specialized Road Traffic Reports whose readership is perhaps not as wide as it should be.

'Senior policemen and MPs are sabre-rattling for more drug-driving laws but framing legislation on the basis of evidence that a drug is present in a person's body will be difficult in practical terms and poses a civil liberties issue. A person can be prosecuted for illegal drug use, but that is not a motoring offence . . . Where's the impairment?' asked Andrew English.

In fact, no such new laws are necessary. If senior police officers and the Crown Prosecution Service had done their homework, they would have known all along that the question does not arise and that impairment can be proved through the application of good, old-fashioned, simple British common sense.

For consider the facts of *Leetham* v. *DPP*, reported in (1999) Road Traffic Reports at page twenty-nine.

At about 11.35 p.m. on Friday, 21 February 1997, a police sergeant and constable were travelling in a marked police patrol car along a road in Sittingbourne, Kent, in a 30-mph speed area. The sergeant, who was driving, had indicated he wanted to turn left but a Honda Accord driven by Robin Leetham, a self-employed engineer, suddenly appeared in front of him coming from the other direction and overtaking another car. The sergeant had to brake sharply to avoid a collision. He promptly turned his car round and chased after the Honda Accord, blue light flashing and sirens screaming. The Honda eventually stopped and the police constable got out and went over to talk to the driver. He could not smell liquor on his breath but noticed that his eyes were red, his speech slurred and his answers were slow. The constable formed the view that he was under the influence of drugs and told him he was going to search him for drugs but the driver volunteered that he had smoked one cannabis cigarette earlier that evening and had some cannabis resin on him, which he produced.

He was taken to Sittingbourne police station where he was seen by a police surgeon who took a blood sample for analysis. A forensic scientist later signed a statement that he had found no alcohol in the blood but a chemical compound arising from the major active ingredients of cannabis/cannabis resin. He could not say when Mr Lee-tham had last used the drug but stated his opinion that 'the effects could include dreamlike euphoria, feelings of relaxation and possible drowsiness, loss of coordination and reduced concentration, which might adversely affect driving'. Such effects begin almost immediately after use, maximize about twenty minutes later and are relatively short-lived, lasting normally around one to two hours or up to about four hours.

On 13 October 1997 Robin Leetham was tried at Sittingbourne Magistrates' Court for driving a mechanically pro-pelled vehicle on a road while unfit to drive through drugs, contrary to Section 4 (1) of the 1988 Act.

The two police officers gave evidence but the police surgeon who took the blood sample was not called nor was the forensic scientist whose statement was by agreement read to the court. Mr Leetham was the only witness for the defence, admitting that he smoked cannabis fairly regularly because it calmed him down and that he had smoked one joint at about 7.00 to 7.30 that night but did not drive until about four hours later by which time he had thought the cannabis would have worn off. He did not dispute that his eyes might have been red but said he had been working twelve-hour days. He also said that he had a deep voice and suffered from dyslexia which slurred his speech at times.

On that evidence, would *you* have convicted him of driving while his ability to do so was impaired? Remember, there was no scientific evidence as to how much cannabis he had taken into his system, no evidence whatsoever from the police surgeon as to his view of any impaired driving ability – and Mr Leetham had given some explanation as to why his eyes were red and his speech slurred. On the other hand, there was the reckless nature of his driving, the police constable's evidence about his demeanour – and the fact that we only have his word that he had smoked just one cannabis cigarette some four hours earlier that evening.

So would *you* have been satisfied beyond reasonable doubt of his guilt?

In fact, the Sittingbourne magistrates convicted him, fined him £250, ordered his licence to be endorsed and disqualified him from driving for three years because – as they discovered only after finding him guilty – this was his second such offence within ten years.

In March 1998 – although the case only found its way
into the Road Traffic Reports nearly a year later! – the
High Court rejected his appeal and upheld the conviction.
Lord Justice Rose, one of the few senior judges today
whose robust common sense is as great as his legal acu-
men, swept aside Mr Leetham's counsel's argument that
medical evidence of impairment should have been called
and that the police constable had gone too far in talking
about his client's red eyes, slurred speech and slow
answers to questions.

'The crucial question in this case,' said Lord Justice Rose,
'is whether there was material, despite the fact that no
doctor was called, which justified the justices in concluding
that the drugs had impaired the defendant's ability properly to drive.'

And he answered his own question with these words:
'In my judgment, they were entitled to look at all the
evidence in the case in relation to the way in which the car
was driven, the consumption of cannabis which the
defendant admitted, the presence of cannabis in his blood
on subsequent analysis, the effects of that drug, in particular, in relation to "feelings of relaxation and possible
drowsiness, loss of coordination and reduced concentration", and to put all that evidence with the evidence
from the police officers as to the slurred and slow character
of the defendant's speech.'

I have to smile, for I have a definite sense of *déjà vu*.
That judgment could have been given back in the Sixties
when convictions for drink-driving were habitually
obtained by police officers telling a judge – and, in those

days, juries – that, as well as smelling alcohol on the
defendant's breath, they had noticed his eyes were blood-
shot, his speech was slurred and he staggered when he
moved. Then and now, common sense does sometimes
prevail in the law.

E

ELDERLY DRIVERS

We have seen under **Age** that there is no legal limit on how old a driver can be and I wrote there of how my own mother-in-law was still driving on public roads at ninety-one. In fact, recent statistics have revealed that, of Britain's 32 million driving-licence holders, 1.9 million are over seventy. Of these, about 2,000 are over ninety.

But who is – or was – Britain's oldest driver?

According to a spokesman for the *Guinness Book of Records*, the country's oldest driver was Edward Newsome from Brighton who was still driving at his 105th birthday: 'But he died in 1997 and we do not have a record for the oldest living driver today.' The spokesman was commenting in June 1999 on the case of Miss Millicent Butler from Crediton, Devon, who taught herself to drive at the age of fourteen and, having recently celebrated her 101st birthday, still enjoyed the 6-mile drive from her home to Exeter for shopping and once a week drove to work as a volunteer steward at Exeter Cathedral. One can imagine the expression on a police officer's face if he ever asked, as a matter of routine, to see her driving licence!

EMERGENCY

When is it a defence to a drink-driving charge that you
had to drive?

The short answer is that no emergency can prevent a
conviction. However, in rare cases, you may save your
licence if magistrates accept that the emergency 'justified'
your driving. That was the word used by Lord Widgery,
then Lord Chief Justice, in *Taylor* v. *Rajan*, in January 1974.
The emergency will then amount to 'special reasons',
allowing magistrates to exercise a discretion not to disqualify, although they usually still impose a fine. Lord Widgery
ruled: 'Justices should approach the exercise of this discretion with great care. The test is not subjective. The
justices should not try to put themselves in the position of
the driver with drink in his body and ask whether it was a
reasonable decision for him to take. The matter must be
considered objectively.'

Mr Justice Leggatt said in the more recent case of *DPP*
v. *Doyle*, in December 1988: 'The decision to refrain from
disqualifying is only to be exercised in clear and compelling circumstances and the burden of proof of those clear
and compelling circumstances lies on the defendant.' But
the essence of the law was stated by Lord Widgery in
Taylor v. Rajan: 'The justices must consider all the circumstances. They must consider the nature and degree of the
crisis or emergency; they must consider with particular
care whether there are alternative means of transport or
methods of dealing with the crisis, other than the use by

the defendant of his own car. They should have regard to the manner in which the defendant drove, because if he committed traffic offences, such as excessive speed or driving without due care and attention, this again is a consideration which tells against his having the discretion exercised in his favour, and they should generally have regard to whether the defendant acted responsibly or otherwise.'

Here are two typical cases where non-disqualification pleas did not succeed. A central London restaurant manager was at home in Richmond, Surrey, on a Saturday night, suffering from flu. He did not expect to go to work and drank some brandy. At 10 p.m. the restaurant staff called to say that the deputy manager had been taken ill and there was no one to lock up. The manager drove to the restaurant in the West End, had no more to drink and locked up at about 12.30 a.m. He drove home but was stopped by police for speeding. He was still well over the limit and he lost his licence because he had not even tried to find an alternative method of travel and had been speeding. Furthermore, as Mr Justice Mackenna shrewdly observed, 'Even if it had been necessary to drive to Curzon Street, which it was not, there is no evidence that it was necessary for him to drive back to Richmond.'

When a woman in Manchester went to retrieve her car from her ex-boyfriend, who had taken it without permission, he assaulted her and damaged the car. She managed to drive to a friend's house and telephoned the police to ask them to meet her at her home just over a mile away. She then drank brandy before driving home, deciding not to walk or get a taxi because she feared the ex-boyfriend would further damage her car if she left it at her friend's. Non-disqualification was refused because, as Lord Justice Rose ruled, a driver should not deliberately decide to drink knowing that he would – or probably would – drive.

So when can a non-disqualification plea prevail? Only when driving is the only practicable alternative and you are not too much over the limit. This happened to a woman in Huntingdon, Cambridgeshire, who left her baby at home with a fourteen-year-old baby-sitter and drove to a pub. She had been receiving threatening phone calls and, when she called home to check all was well, the baby-sitter reported several more and pleaded with her to return.

The woman's attempts to get a taxi were unsuccessful so, although she had drunk one and a half pints of cider, she drove home and was stopped while just over the limit. 'This was as clear and compelling an example as could be contemplated of a crisis or emergency which moved the defendant to use her car,' said Mr Justice Leggatt in upholding the magistrates' refusal to disqualify. It really must be as extreme as that.

EXTENDED WARRANTIES

Are they worth paying extra money for?

To my mind, it depends on the cost and wording of the specific warranty and, even more, on the *calibre* of the vehicle.

Let me explain. Instead of the old provision in Section 14 of the 1979 Sale of Goods Act that goods had to be of 'merchantable quality' – a highly legalistic phrase without any immediately apparent meaning – this was amended by the Sale and Supply of Goods Act in 1994 to say that goods must be of *satisfactory* quality'.

And the 1994 Act spells out, in surprisingly everyday language, what 'satisfactory' means: 'Goods are of satisfactory quality if they meet the standard that a reasonable person would regard as satisfactory, taking account of any description, the price (if relevant) and all the other relevant circumstances.' It continues: 'For the purposes of this Act, quality includes ... durability.' But it does not define 'durability' and gives no period for which goods are supposed to remain durable.

How could it, though? Different types of goods will last for different lengths of time and, even with the same type (e.g. a motor car), there will be wildly differing periods depending (primarily) on cost.

So one is thrown back on that traditional stand-by of the law: reasonableness. You are entitled to expect that your car, and its individual components, will last for a *reasonable* length of time.

But I regret that I cannot point to a single High Court or Appeal Court case decided under the new Act in which a judge gives authoritative assistance in determining what 'durability' may mean in any particular instance. Nor is this surprising. I can well believe that, if a case looked like going the motorist's way before it got to court, the manufacturer would settle and so avoid a legal precedent being set.

But that does not mean that we are without any kind of judicial guidance, and I would refer to the case of *Rogers* v. *Parish (Scarborough) Ltd* decided in the Court of Appeal in November 1986. Admittedly, this was a case brought under the old law. The Court ruled that a Yorkshire businessman was entitled after six months to reject, as not of 'merchantable quality', a new Range Rover bought in 1981 for £16,000. It had had persistent and grievous troubles with its engine, gear-box, body and oil seals.

And Lord Justice Mustill said, 'The description "Range Rover" would conjure up a particular set of expectations, not the same as those relating to an ordinary saloon car, as to the balance between performance, handling, comfort and resilience. The factor of price was also significant. At more than £16,000 [at 1981 prices!], this vehicle was, if not at the top of the scale, well above the level of the ordinary family saloon. The buyer was entitled to value for his money.'

I am convinced that similar reasoning would apply to deciding the issue of 'durability' under the 1994 Act. Any reasonable motorist – or judge – would expect a brand-new Rolls-Royce or Mercedes costing tens of thousands of pounds to last longer than a small family saloon costing only a fraction of that price.

With cars, as with so much else in this world, you get what you pay for.

F

FAIRNESS

We have already seen under **Breath Tests** that if a breath sample taken at a police station after a positive roadside breath test shows more than 35 µg of alcohol in 100 ml of breath (the legal limit) but less than 50 µg, the police must offer the choice of a replacement sample of either blood or urine – which the police have the right to select.

This provision of Section 8 of the 1988 Road Traffic Act is to ensure fairness in such cases to drivers who are thus offered an alternative way of establishing exactly how much alcohol is in their body. But what if a motorist is too befuddled to make this choice? Should the first reading stand so as to ensure his conviction or can he successfully argue that his genuine inability to accept the offer of a new sample vitiates the whole process?

The question arose in the High Court in 1995 in the case of *DPP* v. *Berry*. What had happened was that Mr Berry, after failing a roadside breath test, gave a breath sample of between 35 and 50 µg at a police station, and so came within the protection of Section 8. Unfortunately, as the Law Report states, 'partly as a consequence of the alcohol he had taken, he was unable to understand the choice available to him'. So no replacement sample was taken.

At Bradford Magistrates' Court, Mr Berry's lawyer argued that, because his client had been unable to understand his rights, he had not had an opportunity to test a sample of blood or urine against the breath specimen. The magistrates agreed, ruled that the breath specimen was inadmissible and, since there was no other proof of the amount of alcohol in his body, acquitted him. But the prosecution appealed and the High Court ruled that Mr Berry had not been deprived of his rights under the 1988 Act. He had, in effect, deprived himself of them and could not be heard to complain about something that was wholly or partly his own fault. As Mr Justice Scott Baker said, 'The clear inference from the facts is that the defendant's consumption of alcohol either caused or contributed to his inability to understand the offer to replace the breath specimen. It should, therefore, have stood in evidence.' The acquittal was overruled, and the case sent back to the magistrates.

To be honest, I would have expected no less. Four years previously, in *DPP* v. *Poole* where a breath reading was 41 µg and a motorist refused to listen to a police officer's explanation of the choice then open to him and walked out of the room, the High Court ruled he was not entitled to be acquitted. It laid down that if a motorist, by his own actions, frustrates a police officer's proper performance of his duty, he cannot expect the only available evidence of his alcoholic intake to be ignored. Common sense sometimes prevails in our courts: even in drink-driving cases.

FIXED PENALTY SYSTEM

This exists to ease the log-jam in the courts and encourage the motorist to accept his guilt by offering him the soft option of a fixed penalty. The court system is bypassed and you pay to the local Fixed Penalty Office a £30 penalty for non-endorsable motoring offences, such as seat-belt or lighting offences, and for parking offences outside London. Or £40 for parking offences in London. Or £60 for Red Route parking offences in London and £60 and three penalty points for all endorsable offences throughout the country, such as speeding or defective tyres. These penalties were increased in October 2000 for the first time in eight years and are now subject to annual review in the light of the Government's Road Safety Strategy announced in March 2000. This set an overall 40 per cent reduction target for the year 2010 in the number of people killed or seriously injured on the roads, with a 50 per cent reduction target for children.

Despite these recent increases, the system really is a good deal. You are *guaranteed* these fixed penalties and fixed points, although (certainly) the fine and (perhaps) the number of points would be more if you took the case to court.

Fixed penalties are not available for the most serious offences, such as careless or dangerous driving or drink-driving, but they cover a wide spectrum of medium-scale offences. In penalty point cases, only a uniformed police officer can hand you a fixed penalty notice and he will only do so if you surrender your driving licence on the spot or within seven days at a police station of your choice *and* he sees that you are not liable for 'totting up'. It also helps to be polite!

If the offence does not carry penalty points, a uniformed police officer or traffic warden can leave the fixed penalty notice attached to your vehicle, usually stuck on your windscreen. In London, Winchester, Oxford and Maidstone, where parking is taken out of the hands of the police and 'decriminalized', it is a local parking attendant who will carry out this duty and issue what is called in those circumstances, a penalty charge notice.

Most motorists believe it is not worthwhile querying either kind of notice. They pay up and save themselves money. Yet it is possible to beat the system. It is pointless challenging the notice on the basis that you have not committed an offence. The Fixed Penalty Clerk will simply write back saying you must let the matter go to court.

What you should do is to write admitting that you were technically guilty but explaining why you think that the ticket was unfair or unjust. Someone in authority will then reply that you should still pay the penalty while your representations are being considered but it will be refunded if ultimately they agree that 'the circumstances do not warrant further proceedings'. You should always comply with such a request, for notices are cancelled and payments refunded in genuine cases of hardship or serious mitigation. Pregnant mothers and elderly drivers are among those who sometimes are treated sympathetically.

But there is another reason why we should all query a

notice: there is always the chance that we will disclose a technical fault. I give an example of my own. At 10.10 on a Monday morning I came downstairs to the mews in Chelsea, London, where I lived in a small block of flats (when the police still handled parking violations in the capital) to move my car into an underground garage – only to find a £30 fixed penalty notice for parking on a single yellow line. I had been unable to put the car into the garage the previous evening because the entrance was blocked by a parked car, and I could not use my £70 local resident's permit because the bays were full of cars displaying no such permit.

So I wrote to the Fixed Penalty Clerk asking if he would take no further action. I received a reply from the Metropolitan Police asking me to pay the penalty while the matter was considered – which I did – and eventually received a further letter saying that the issue of the notice had been 'correct in the circumstances'. However, the police said they would still ask the clerk to return my cheque because the issuing officer had made an 'administrative error'.

This error – omitting details of the parking restrictions – was only spotted because I had queried the notice. A friendly council official explained: 'When mitigation is received from a member of the public, the fixed penalty notice is checked. If it is then noted that the notice was incorrectly completed by the issuing officer, it is cancelled.'

You never know your luck!

G

GARAGES

Cowboys are not only to be found on the plains of the American Wild West. In August 2000, the Office of Fair Trading released a report, based on extensive research over different areas of the country, which told motorists what many of us have known for years: that too many garages are rip-off merchants cheating us on a devastating scale.

The report highlighted that shoddy or unnecessary work leads to 1.3 million complaints a year and costs consumers £170 million: an average of £130 per case. But that may be 'only the tip of the iceberg' because many sub-standard repairs go unreported by motorists who lack the technical knowledge to challenge what has been done – or not done.

John Bridgeman, then Director General of Fair Trading, said his Office's research showed that the quality of a lot of car repair work was 'unacceptable'. He said, 'Our overall verdict on the service provided by many large firms, franchised dealers and local garages is that it is unroadworthy and needs a thorough overhaul. Not many of us have enough expertise to check if a competent or even adequate job has been done, and we are at the mercy of people who are supposed to know what they are doing. I'm afraid this trust is often misplaced.'

An analysis of checks by local trading standards officers suggested that the proportion of 'critically unsatisfactory' repairs and servicing work could be as high as 39 per cent, some of which involved clear accident risks. Random inspections of seventy-seven garages in four areas had uncovered twenty where services were so poor that prosecutions had ensued or were still being considered. A further ten received warnings.

The report called for a working group of Government, consumer and industry representatives to examine ways of improving staff training and service quality, and lay down new standards for consumer information and handling of complaints. But we should not hold our breath. Stephen Byers, the Trade and Industry Secretary, commented that the findings were 'disturbing' and promised to consider the proposals 'as a matter of urgency'. He did not promise to do anything so positive as actually to implement them.

For its part, the Retail Motor Industry Federation, representing about 10,000 garages, made bland, vaguely reassuring noises. It expressed support for the idea of greater monitoring of the industry and said that it welcomed the report 'for exposing disreputable and unscrupulous garages that bring down the good name of the reputable and respectable trade'.

GETTING BACK YOUR LICENCE

One of the first questions asked by motorists who are so
unfortunate as to lose their licence is: 'When can I ask to
get it back?' The answer is contained in Section 42 of the
1988 Road Offenders Act and is perhaps a little disappoint-
ing. You have to go back to the court that imposed the
disqualification – but you cannot do so for at least two
years. So anyone banned for less than two years can never
hope to get it back ahead of time. This situation is made
even more daunting by the fact that most bans are for only
twelve or eighteen months! In fact, you must wait at least
two years for a four-year disqualification, half the total
time if it is for four to ten years, and five years for any
longer ban. The only exception is that anyone disqualified
for three years or more because of a *second* drink-driving
conviction may apply for its removal after the halfway
mark. But even if you are within the proper time-scale, the
prospects of success are slim. Section 42 merely states: 'The
court may, if it thinks proper having regard to (a) the
character of the person disqualified and his conduct subsequent to the order, (b) the nature of the offence, and (c)
any other circumstances of the case remove the disqualification or refuse the application.' In practice, you must have
an almost overwhelming case before you can even think of
possible victory. The police have to be told of your application and nearly always oppose it. In the rare instances
when they support it – generally on compassionate
grounds where, for example, a motorist needs his car to

ferry his seriously ill wife to and from medical treatment –
an application will succeed. Otherwise, the ban will generally be allowed to continue.

'GREENER' CARS

Traditionally cars are assessed for vehicle excise duty (see
Tax Disc) according to engine size, with owners of smaller
cars (engines of 1,100 cc or less) paying at a reduced rate.
But as from 1 March, 2001, the duty on all new cars is
based primarily on their emissions of carbon dioxide,
which is a major 'greenhouse' gas. The fewer the emissions,
the less is the duty you pay. In the words of the DVLA's
explanatory leaflet, 'The new system will send a clear
signal to vehicle manufacturers and purchasers about the
environmental impact of the cars they make and use, and
will encourage the use of more fuel-efficient cars.' It is to
be hoped that it works out that way.

H

HEADLIGHT FLASHING

What offence, if any, do you commit in flashing your headlights to warn an oncoming speeding motorist that there is a police speed trap ahead – as I saw recently on the M40? Surely you are merely telling your fellow drivers to stop breaking the law, and how can that be wrong?

The judges are not that naive. As far back as 1910 the High Court upheld the conviction of an AA patrolman who had warned drivers exceeding the then legal limit of 20 mph that they were approaching a police trap. Mr Justice Darling ridiculed the argument that the motorists were simply being told to stop committing the crime of speeding. He said, 'The warning is given in order that the commission of the crime should be suspended while there is danger of detection, with the intention that its commission should be recommenced as soon as the danger of detection is past.'

So what was the offence for which the AA man's conviction was upheld? It was the general offence of wilfully obstructing the police in the lawful execution of their duty. In the words of *Butterworths' Police Law*: 'To "obstruct" is to do any act which prevents or makes it more difficult for a constable to carry out his duty.'

And this applies to police trying to catch motoring law offenders in the same way as any other kind of lawbreaker. As Lord Justice Donaldson commented in a 1981 case, 'Police constables maintain the Queen's Peace in many different ways besides by criminal investigation. They patrol beats. They direct traffic. Is it really to be said that a police constable on point duty is not acting in the execution of his duty? Of course not.' Indeed, a forty-eight-year-old company director, who had never appeared in court before, was fined £150 with £34 costs for flashing his lights at oncoming cars to warn them of a police trap on the A50 near Wigston, Leicestershire. He admitted obstructing the police in the execution of their duty but later described the decision to prosecute him as 'diabolical', adding the time-honoured phrase of motorists in trouble with the law: 'The police could better spend their time catching real criminals.'

He should perhaps have counted himself lucky. Under Section 89 of the 1996 Police Act, he could have been jailed for up to a month or fined up to £1,000 – or both.

HIGHWAY CODE

Not many people know the Highway Code's exact legal status. It does *not* create offences in itself, but breach of its provisions can be used to help prove that a criminal offence has been committed or civil liability has been incurred.

For instance, Paragraph 88 of the latest (1998) edition of the Code states: 'You MUST obey all traffic light signals and traffic signs giving orders, including temporary signals and signs. Make sure you know, understand and act on all other traffic and information signs and road markings.' That is both good general advice and also a potent warning.

If you do not comply with those requirements, that can go towards proving that you have committed offences against Section 36 of the 1988 Road Traffic Act or the 1994 Traffic Signs Regulations or the 1994 Traffic Signs General Directions, for which you could be fined in a criminal court, *and* have driven with such lack of reasonable care as to be held liable in a civil court to pay compensation for your negligence.

The Highway Code is not law but its breach goes a long way towards proving that you have broken the law.

HIRE PURCHASE

Normally anyone buying goods on hire purchase has no legal right to sell them until they are fully paid off: they still belong to the finance company. But the 1974 Consumer Credit Act states that a private person (not a dealer) who buys a car, motorcycle or other motor vehicle for £15,000 or less without knowing of the existence of a hire purchase agreement or without knowing that such an agreement has not been paid off, gets a good legal title, even though, as always with hire purchase, the car was not the hire purchaser's to sell but still remained (until the very last payment) the property of the finance company. In such a case, the company's sole recourse is against their own customer – if they can find him and he is worth pursuing through the courts.

But that is not all. A dealer, even though innocent, will not get good title but, if he sells on to an innocent person, that private person will become the new legal owner. It is only the dealer who is penalized. That is why, in practice, dealers usually check with a company set up by the finance companies, called HPI (Hire Purchase Information), which has a database of all current motor-vehicle hire purchase agreements.

HIT AND RUN

The term 'hit and run' does not only apply to those cases where a driver causes death or injury to an individual and drives on without stopping, where, as we will see under **Motor Insurers' Bureau**, the victim can get compensation with the help of the Bureau. The term is also appropriate where a motorist scrapes or otherwise damages a parked car while trying to park his own vehicle and then drives off without leaving a note – as all too often happens. In this type of case, where there is only damage to property, the victim cannot appeal to the Bureau. He will either have to pay for the damage out of his own pocket or make a

claim on his own insurance company, if covered (see
Insurance.)

HOLIDAY DRIVING IN THE UK

Millions of motorists every year take their cars to drive on
holiday abroad (see **Overseas Driving**) but many more use
their cars to holiday in Britain. So it may be of interest to
examine some of the legal hazards they may encounter.

Slow-moving country traffic

Driving too slowly is not an offence in itself. It is *how* one
drives slowly that is important. An elderly motorist
worried about going too fast in a narrow country lane or a
farm-tractor driver or motorist towing a caravan on an
ordinary country road should, if at all possible, pull over
to let other drivers pass. If not, they may be guilty of
driving without reasonable consideration for other road
users.

So at Wells Magistrates' Court a thirty-three-year-old
farm worker who drove a combine harvester at 5–10 miles
an hour on the A361 in Somerset on a mid-morning in
August and caused a queue of frustrated drivers to build
up behind him was fined £120 with £200 costs and had his
licence endorsed. The court clerk said with some feeling,
'He drove for one and a half miles without stopping to
allow a very long queue of traffic to overtake. He could
have used the lay-bys to allow the traffic to get by.'

That last remark contains the essence of the law. It is a slow-moving motorist's obstinate refusal to let other drivers pass when it is safe or reasonable for them to do so that makes this form of driving criminal.

Paragraph 145 of the Highway Code clearly lays down: 'Do not hold up a long queue of traffic, especially if you are driving a large or slow-moving vehicle. Check your mirrors frequently, and, if necessary, pull in where it is safe and let traffic pass.

Temporary traffic lights at roadworks

What is the legal status of temporary traffic lights? Some motorists believe that even when they are showing red, you do not have to stop if you can safely see your way ahead. That is simply not so. The 1994 Traffic Signs Regulations and General Directions give portable temporary lights at road works and temporary road traffic-control schemes equal validity with permanent traffic lights. If they show red, you must stop – even if the way ahead is clear.

(See also under **Traffic Lights**.)

Roof racks

If you carry anything on a roof rack it must be securely fixed, because if it comes off you may be prosecuted for having an unsafe load. It is no defence that you took *some* precautions. You commit the offence if the load is unsafe, whatever precautions you may have taken.

Horse riders

Always give horse riders a wide berth. As the Highway Code says, 'Be particularly careful of horses and riders, especially when overtaking. Always pass wide and slow. Horse riders are often children, so take extra care and remember riders may ride in double file when escorting a young or inexperienced horse rider. Look out for horse riders' signals and heed a request to slow down or stop. Treat all horses as a potential hazard and take great care.'

Motorways (and hard shoulders)

Most of us know something about the special legal rules that apply to motorways: no learner drivers, tractors, cyclists or moped riders, no picking up or setting down of passengers, etc. But the following three situations may cause particular problems.

Leaving the motorway

Do not, like so many drivers, suddenly pull off an outside lane in front of drivers in the nearside left-hand lane who then may have to brake sharply. If a police patrol were to see you do this, you could be warned about inconsiderate driving.

What is an emergency entitling you to pull on to the hard shoulder?

Regulation 7 of the 1982 Motorways Traffic (England and Wales) Regulations says you can stop on a hard shoulder 'by reason of any accident, illness or other emergency' but – of course! – does not say what constitutes an emergency.

Fortunately the late Lord Widgery, when Lord Chief Justice, filled that gap. It was in a case where a tired motorist had pulled on to the hard shoulder because he thought that it was no longer safe to continue driving. Starting from the dictionary definition of emergency as 'a sudden and/or unexpected occurrence', Lord Widgery said, 'Too much stress must not be attached to the word "sudden".' The tiredness does not have to attack the motorist at the very second before he pulls on to the hard shoulder. 'If he gets on to the carriageway at a time when, so far as he could see, it was safe and lawful for him to proceed to the the next turn-off point, it is sufficient to show that something intervened which rendered it unsafe to proceed to that next turn-off point.' (See also **Queasy or Tired**.)

A child suddenly being sick or needing the loo, or an urgent call of nature on your own part, making it impossible for you as the driver to concentrate properly on driving, *could* be an emergency entitling you to pull over and stop on the hard shoulder – but you would have to persuade a police officer that you had had no prior warning of any such event before you passed the last exit! In October 1999, Sir Alex Ferguson, the Manchester United manager, did not tell a policeman why he had chosen to drive along the hard shoulder of the 602, where there was a long traffic jam, so that he could reach the M62 and return to Old Trafford because, as he later told Bury Magistrates' Court, he was concerned about the publicity and the embarrassment. In fact, he was suffering from severe diarrhoea and, as he said graphically in the witness box, 'I had to go somewhere quickly.' The sympathetic magistrates accepted that was an 'emergency' and acquitted him of 'using' the motorway's hard shoulder, contrary to Regulation 9 of the 1981 Regulations where use in an emergency is similarly permitted.

Can you lawfully make a U-turn on the motorway to go back the other way and avoid a long traffic jam ahead?
Don't be tempted. It is legally too risky. You can be fined up to £2,500, have your licence endorsed with three to six penalty points and face discretionary disqualification for breach of Regulation 10 of the 1982 Regulations. It could even amount to careless or dangerous driving.

(See also **U-turn**.)

Hotel car parks

If your car is stolen from a hotel car park, the hotel will not be liable unless you can prove they were negligent. This is usually very difficult. Some country hotels have a sign in their rooms saying that goods should not be left on display in parked cars. Why should they do that? There has probably been recent pilfering of goods from parked cars and, if they did not warn motorists, they could be held liable in negligence.

HOME

Are the police obliged to stop at the door? When can the police breath-test you for alleged drink-driving, once you have got back home?

The question is simple. The answer, however, is complex because some judges and magistrates have never liked the idea of home tests ever since the 1967 Road Safety Act brought the breath test into motoring law. As Lord Scarman has said, 'Parliament must be understood, even in its desire to stamp out drunken driving, to pay respect to the fundamental right of privacy in one's own home, which has for centuries been recognized by the common law.' After all, it was a judge (Chief Justice Coke) who first said in the early seventeenth century, 'An Englishman's home is his castle.'

Two basic legal propositions are easy and straightforward.

If you were involved in an accident in which someone else was injured (not just yourself), a uniformed policeman can enter your home, by force if necessary, and request a breath test, with the normal consequences of arrest, fine and disqualification if you refuse.

If, at a less serious level, a uniformed policeman merely has reasonable cause to believe that, while driving, you had alcohol in your body or committed a moving traffic offence, he can knock on your door and request a breath test on your doorstep or, if you let him into your house, request the test inside – again, with the usual consequences for refusal. The difficulties start if you do not let him in or, once inside, you

ask him to leave. As any experienced police officer knows
(but may not be prepared to admit), that puts him in a very
sensitive legal position. If he persists with his request, and
you refuse, he can undoubtedly arrest you on the spot, take
you to a police station and, if you then prove positive,
charge you with drink-driving. The arrest will have been
unlawful because he was a trespasser – but the House of
Lords ruled in October 1985 that that does not matter. 'A
lawful arrest is not an essential prerequisite of a breath test,'
said Lord Fraser of Tullybelton.

But he added, 'If a motorist has been lured to the police
station by some trick or deception, or if the police officers
have behaved oppressively', a court has a discretion to
throw out the charge. This did not apply in that case
because the local police (in Gwent) had merely made 'a
bona fide mistake as to their powers'.

Lord Fraser's words, echoed by his fellow Law Lords,
have become the basis for a defence of 'oppressive behaviour' that is comparatively little known but has, on
occasions, proved remarkably successful, especially since
the case of *Matto* v. *Wolverhampton Crown Court* in 1987, in
which the High Court quashed a motorist's conviction. He
had told police they could not test him on his own drive-
way, and they had high-handedly replied, 'We know what
we are doing. If I wrongfully arrest you, you can sue me.
OK?' Lord Justice Woolf ruled that was 'behaving in an
oppressive manner'.

A case at Grays Magistrates' Court in Essex typifies the
courts' readiness to curb possible police excess. The driver
of a police car told the Bench how, on seeing a woman

motorist hit a kerb, he had chased her home, obtained access to her house – and breath-tested her in her own bedroom. When he entered the room, she was lying under the blankets claiming to have flu but she was fully clothed and her breath smelt of alcohol and her speech was slurred.

That was suspicious enough but the vital legal question was: how had the police officer obtained access to the house? He said that the woman's seventeen-year-old daughter had let him in. He denied defence counsel's accusation that he had tricked his way in by 'telling her you were going to go in anyway – when you had no power to do so'. 'I was really looking for an invite into the house,' the officer replied. 'I didn't want to intimidate her. I am not that sort of officer.' But the prosecuting solicitor told the Bench, 'In the circumstances, I am not prepared to continue with this case,' and the magistrates awarded the defendant her costs.

HOSPITAL

I would like you to consider this set of facts. There has been an accident on a motorway in the early hours of the morning. One of the two drivers involved is rushed into intensive care at a local hospital suffering from head and facial injuries. Two hours later, at about 5.00, a uniformed police officer arrives and, suspecting that the injured driver was over the legal alcohol limit at the time of the accident, obtains the registrar's permission to see him and request a blood specimen for analysis. After introducing himself, and with a police surgeon present, the officer then tells the driver in the stilted language beloved of the police force, 'I require you to provide a specimen of your blood or urine for a laboratory test. Your refusal to provide this specimen may make you liable to prosecution. Will you give such a specimen?' The driver nods his agreement.

The police officer then says, 'I propose that the specimen be of blood, unless you state that there is a medical reason why this should not be so.' The driver says, 'Yes.' The police surgeon takes a specimen, which is found to contain 135 mg of alcohol to 100 ml of blood, well over the legal limit of 80 mg. And that is several hours after the accident.

Do you see anything wrong in that procedure? Do you think the motorist has any chance of avoiding a drink-driving conviction and losing his licence? Most drivers, perhaps even some non-specialist lawyers, would probably say 'No' to both questions. In fact, due to a High Court ruling in *DPP* v. *Duffy*, they would be wrong. Two judges decided that Wakefield magistrates had correctly dismissed a drink-driving charge against the somewhat fortunate Mr Duffy, involved in an early-morning M1 accident in those circumstances.

Why? Where had the Yorkshire policeman gone wrong? Normally, the 1988 Road Traffic Act states that a driver can only be asked for a definitive breath, blood or urine test if a screening breath test has first proved positive at the roadside. But one exception is when an injured driver has been taken off to hospital.

Strictly speaking, a policeman does not then need to administer a screening breath test. He can at once, with the permission of the doctor in charge, ask the injured motorist for a definitive blood or urine sample for analysis. The 1992 House of Lords' case of *DPP* v. *Warren* has made clear that it is the police officer's decision whether to ask for blood or urine. But that is not all. As Lord Bridge said, 'If the constable decides to require blood, [he must] ask the driver if there are any reasons why a specimen cannot or should not be taken by a doctor. This will give the driver the opportunity to raise any objection he may have to giving blood, either on medical grounds or for any other reason which might afford a "reasonable excuse".'

That was what went wrong in *DPP* v. *Duffy*. The policeman told Mr Duffy that he was going to ask the police surgeon to take a specimen of blood 'unless you state that there is a medical reason why this should not be so'; but the High Court ruled that was not good enough. He should have specifically asked him: 'Are there any reasons why a specimen of blood could not or should not be taken?' A police officer does not have to specify if there are any medical reasons for not taking blood. He merely has to ask if there are any reasons. But he must do exactly that. He cannot just allude to it. He must spell it out. If he does not, the motorist is entitled to be acquitted. Many people may think this is all playing with words – but whoever said that justice is always the same as the law?

HUMAN RIGHTS

By now, everyone in the country must know that in October 2000 the European Human Rights Convention, having been partly adopted into Scottish law a year before, became fully integrated into English law. The Government spent millions of pounds on massive publicity and on gearing the legal world to this – to many – unwarranted intrusion into our traditional system of justice.

But what effect is it likely to have on motoring law? Section 3 of the 1998 Human Rights Act provides an escape clause for courts facing a dilemma as to whether existing law complies with the Convention. The Section requires our legislation to be interpreted in a way that is compatible with the Convention, 'so far as it is possible to do so'. That wording is a typical Blair Government fudge, but already there are ominous signs that the Act is going to have a major and not always beneficial impact.

The basic 'human rights', as laid out in the Convention and repeated in the First Schedule to the 1998 Act, are: Article 2: Right to life; Article 3: Prohibition of torture; Article 4: Prohibition of slavery and forced labour; Article 5: Right to liberty and security; Article 6: Right to a fair trial; Article 7: No punishment without law; Article 8: Right to respect for private and family life; Article 9: Freedom of thought and conscience and religion; Article 10: Freedom of expression; Article 11: Freedom of assembly and association (covering trade unions); Article 12: Right to marry; Article 13: Prohibition of discrimination.

In motoring-law terms, the Articles with the biggest effect are likely to be 6 and 8. The latter Article is relevant because it provides a potential beanfeast for defence lawyers arguing in drink-driving cases that the compulsory taking of breath tests or urine and blood samples offends against the right to respect for one's private life.

This is still early days and so far I know of no case where Article 8 has been successfully invoked in an attempt to thwart a prosecution. But Article 6 has already prompted two highly controversial decisions: one in Scotland and the other in Birmingham (with a judge in July anticipating ahead of time the Convention's incorporation into English law).

The Scottish case, in February 2000, involved a woman named Margaret Brown who was charged in Dunfermline with drink-driving. She was over the blood alcohol limit but was cleared after her lawyer argued that when the police had stopped and asked her in a superstore car park if she had driven her car there, that infringed her right to a fair trial. The police were merely using their everyday power given to them by Section 172 of the 1988 Road Traffic Act to ask, both in England and Scotland, the 'keeper' of a motor vehicle 'such information as to the identity of the driver as they may require' when investigating the alleged commission of an offence. Lord Rodger of Earlsferry, the Lord Justice General and Scotland's most senior judge, ruled that, by compelling her to say who had driven her car the police had forced her to incriminate herself, which breached Article 6 because it is an essential element of a fair trial that anyone suspected of a crime is entitled to remain silent so as not to incriminate themselves. The Dunfermline procurator fiscal appealed to the Privy Council which, since Scottish Devolution, is no longer only the ultimate court of appeal from many parts of the Commonwealth, but also the supreme court for the whole of Great Britain. Until the results of that appeal, the law both north and south of the Border remained uncertain. Although police in Scotland continued to question motorists despite Lord Rodger of Earlsferry's ruling, solicitors in both Scotland and England advised clients facing motoring charges where the identity of the driver is in question to seek postponements and wait for the Privy Council decision.

The Article 6 case in Birmingham involved cars racing round streets in the city centre. Some drivers had been stopped by the police but two others were caught on video by police surveillance cameras. It was agreed that there was a prima facie case of dangerous driving against both of them. But because their identities had only been established by the police sending a notice of intended prosecution to the registered keepers of the two cars, as routinely happens in accordance with Section 172 of the 1988 Act, Judge Peter Crawford ruled at Birmingham Crown Court that the evidence of identity must be excluded because it had been obtained in a way that infringed the defendants' rights against self-incrimination – the same flaw as invalidated the proceedings against Margaret Brown in Dunfermline.

The Crown Prosecution Service decided not to appeal against this ruling because there were 'particular factors in the case' and Judge Crawford's ruling, being only that of a circuit judge, did not have the same status as Lord Rodger of Earlsferry's judgment. But in December 2000, the Privy Council gave its eagerly expected ruling in Miss Brown's appeal from Lord Rodger of Earlsferry's decision. It overruled this distinguished Scottish judge and freed motoring law from slavish adherence to the tenets of the Convention. It held that the requirements of Article 6 are not to be treated as absolute. In the words of Lord Bingham of Cornhill: 'Limited qualifications of these rights is acceptable, if reasonably directed by national authorities towards a clear and proper public objective and if representing no greater qualification than the situation calls for'.

He concluded that the need to address the high incidence of death and injury on the roads caused by the misuse of motor vehicles was such that Section 172 did not represent a disproportionate response to that 'serious social problem'.

In other words, common sense prevailed.

ICY ROADS

Is there a legal duty on local councils to grit icy roads? The question is simple. The answer, as so often in the law, is not. It all turns on the proper interpretation of the 1980 Highway Act – which remains unclear. In 1994, Norfolk County Council's insurers paid £300,000 in an out-of-court settlement (and an estimated £100,000 costs) to a driver who had suffered severe brain damage after his car skidded on ice on the A134 trunk road between Thetford and King's Lynn and hit an oncoming lorry. The insurers paid up rather than risk a High Court judgment against the council.

Mr John Chapman, solicitor for the council and its insurers, said their defence would have revolved around the fact that the council, as the local highway authority, had gritted the road, *even though it did not have a statutory duty to do so* (my italics). And they would also have argued that 'it was the driver's fault because he lost control of his car that morning when nobody else on the road had'.

For his part, the driver was quoted as being 'happy' to accept the lesser sum rather than hold out for the full compensation that his own advisers were said to have estimated as worth up to £1 million. So what is the law?

Are highway authorities under a statutory duty, in bad weather, to grit potentially dangerous local roads – or not? The relevant statute is the 1980 Highway Act and it is true that it says nothing whatsoever about highway authorities having to grit icy local roads. All it says (in Section 41) is that the local highway authority 'is under a duty to maintain the highway' and (in Section 58) that it is a defence for the authority to prove that it had taken reasonable care to ensure the highway was not dangerous (see also **Roads** and **Winter Driving**).

But what does that vital word 'maintain' mean in Section 41? We have to go back to the Appeal Court case of *Haydon* v. *Kent County Council*, decided three years before the 1980 Act – but on the same wording in an earlier Act – to try to find the answer. A woman living in Kent had slipped and injured herself on an icy, steep, narrow footpath, walking to work during a February cold snap shortly before Kent County Council, alerted that very morning by a council employee, had gritted the surface.

Could she sue for breach of the council's duty to maintain the footpath? Mr Justice O'Connor awarded her £4,250 damages but the Appeal Court overruled him. And here comes the legal difficulty: there were two different reasons for the decision. Lord Denning, as Master of the Rolls, the presiding judge, ruled there was no liability because the statutory duty to 'maintain' a road does not apply to a mere 'transient obstruction, caused, for example, by snow and ice, which had not damaged the surface of the highway'.

With his immense personal authority, he usually carried

the two other members of the court with him. But not on this occasion. Lord Justices Goff and Shaw agreed that the claim must fail – but only because they ruled that the defence in Section 58 applied and the council had taken reasonable care 'in all the circumstances'. Somewhat reluctantly, they disagreed with their senior judicial colleague. They ruled there was no exception to the general rule for so-called 'transient obstructions'. In Lord Justice Goff's words: 'The statutory obligation to maintain does include clearing snow and ice or providing temporary protection by gritting.'

But which view prevails today: that of Lord Denning or of the two Lords Justices? I cannot tell you. There simply has been no subsequent reported case on similar facts in either the High Court or the Appeal Court to give us an authoritative, clear-cut ruling. Of course, prudent highway authorities continue to grit icy roads whenever reasonably practical – but no one knows if legally they really have to. Many people might find that rather odd.

NOTE: The above entry was written in February 1996. Sadly, and to the detriment of motorists' rights, it has been completely overtaken by events. In June 2000, in *Goodes* v. *East Sussex County Council*, five Law Lords unanimously overruled the Appeal Court decision in *Haydon* v. *Kent County Council* that had stood for over twenty years and laid down that, despite Section 41's clear wording and the fact that a driver had been 'almost entirely paralysed' after his car skidded on an ice patch, councils in England and Wales are under no statutory duty to salt or grit icy roads. In every other instance where subsequent legal events have made my original 'Street Legal' out of date I have revised the text, but here I have kept it in full in order to show how the judges have been less than adequate in their defence of the motorist. Lord Hoffman, who gave the leading judgment, frankly admitted that the law in Scotland is – yet again! – superior to its counterpart south of the Border and that the 1984 Roads (Scotland) Act imposes on local authorities an undoubted legal duty to clear snow and ice from Scottish roads.

He then went on to say, in words that I think the motoring public should be aware of, 'It might be thought that there should be liability upon a highway authority in England and Wales for damages in the event of injury occurring through a failure to take sufficient measures to prevent the safety of the highways under conditions of ice and snow. But there is no remedy there available at Common Law and, if the statute is construed in the way I have preferred, there is no remedy to involve a remedy under the statute. Attempts to achieve such a result by construction seem to me to involve a straining of the statutory language beyond what it can reasonably bear. If a remedy, with the financial consequences which it may involve, is desired, that is a matter for Parliament.'

'I DID NOT SEE IT COMING!'

I have a 'You Are the Judge' poser for you. It is a little before 7.00 on a November morning and a motorist is driving his Ford motor car to work at about 50 mph along a wide, straight road at Barking on the outskirts of East London. We do not know the official street limit but he is travelling too fast for that stretch of road at that time.

Ahead on his side of the road the woman driver of a Lada has just dropped off some passengers and is executing a U-turn in the Ford's path. A parked lorry is partially blocking her view and the Ford driver has time only to brake very hard – witnesses hear the screech of his tyres – before his vehicle smashes into the Lada. Both cars are badly damaged and the Lada driver is injured.

Both admit that neither saw the other before the accident.

he Ford driver, backed by his insurance company, sues the Lada driver for damages, claiming that she is entirely responsible for the crash. Supported by her insurers, she counterclaims that it is all his fault.

You are the judge: who is to blame?

At Barnet County Court in April 1998, in the case on which these facts are based, Judge Peter Latham ruled that the Lada driver was entirely at fault. She lost her counter-claim and she, or rather her insurance company, had to pay all of the Ford driver's claim.

But she appealed and a year later two Appeal Court judges overturned Judge Latham's ruling and said that both drivers were equally to blame. In consequence, the Lada driver's insurers had to pay 50 per cent of the Ford driver's claim, and vice versa.

Lord Justice Sedley's judgment should be priority read-ing for all motorists who automatically say, after an acci-dent, that their driving was impeccable and that the mishap was entirely the other driver's fault.

'It seems to me,' he said, 'that we are left with the elementary position that, in a situation in which each party should have seen the other if they were exercising due care, neither did so ... [This was] a collision which occurred for two reasons. One was that the defendant embarked upon a U-turn without looking either at the moment before she set out or as she began to turn and still had time to stop if anything appeared. The other was that the plaintiff was approaching too fast and without adequate attention to what others were doing on the road. Put in terms of negligence, the defendant created the danger of a collision and the plaintiff failed to avoid it. In these circumstances it seems to me that the blame falls equally on both parties.'

With respect, that is not only good sense but also good law. As far back as 1809, nearly eighty years before the motor car was invented, Lord Ellenborough, a Lord Chief Justice more famous for transporting criminals to Australia, laid down: 'One person being in fault will not dispense with another's using ordinary care for himself.'

In modern law, this principle extensively applies so that, even if one driver is guilty of negligence, that does not prevent another driver from also being guilty of 'contributory negligence' in not taking reasonable care for his or her own safety. Every working day in the County Courts, judges are apportioning the degree of *shared* blame between two drivers after an accident and dividing the damages awarded on that basis.

Of course, many accidents occur where only one motorist has been at fault and the other entirely blameless, but on our crowded roads that is less frequent than previously. The Appeal Court used to discourage appeals that a county court judge had got the proportions wrong in his assessment of blame. The appeal judges said that the best person to decide that issue was the judge who heard the evidence and formed his own view of the witnesses.

In a case of my own many years ago, my client was held 10 per cent to blame for an accident and, as a young barrister, I allowed my heart to rule my head and encouraged him to appeal – with the result that the Appeal Court tersely threw the case out on the basis that I should not trouble them with such trivia. But nowadays appeals against findings of blame even so small as that have become not uncommon.

To help give the feel of this part of the law, here are two typical cases.

A driver was turning right on to a major road from a minor road but a motor cyclist was overtaking stationary traffic on the major road which had stopped to let the driver of the car complete her manoeuvre. The front wheel of the motorcycle struck the offside front of the car turning right. At Staines County Court, Judge Bishop ruled that the motorcyclist was 80 per cent to blame and the car driver 20 per cent.

A minibus driver had emerged from a garage up to halfway across the nearside half of a main road and was waiting to turn left. He beckoned the driver of a car waiting to turn right on to the road from a side road immediately to his left, indicating it was safe to do so. That driver could not see traffic approaching from the right because of the minibus in the middle of the road. Nevertheless, he pulled out around the minibus and collided with a car overtaking the minibus at 30 mph. At Reigate County Court, District Judge Keogh ruled that all three drivers were one-third to blame! He said the overtaking driver was not sufficiently cautious when passing the stationary minibus. The driver of the car that pulled out, though beckoned by the minibus driver, should have 'nosed out' and not assumed the main road was clear simply because the minibus driver had, in effect, told him so, and the minibus driver himself was at fault because he should not have given a signal that the road was clear when it was not. King Solomon could not have done better!

Even motorists whose actual driving is without fault can still have their damages cut because they have not taken reasonable care for their own safety by not wearing a seat-belt. As Lord Denning ruled back in 1975, if wearing a seat-belt would have saved the driver from *all* injury, his or her damages will be cut by 25 per cent and by 15 per cent if the injuries would have been 'a good deal less severe'.

The same applies when an adult passenger has not chosen to belt up. Their 'contributory negligence' can cost them 25 per cent or 15 per cent of the compensation that otherwise would have been their right.

None of us has a monopoly of virtue. In motoring law, as in life, we are each responsible for our own failings (see **Accidents** and **Careless Driving**).

INSURANCE

Section 143 of the 1988 Road Traffic Act makes it a serious offence to use a car on a road without insurance. It lays down a maximum £5,000 fine, endorsement with six to eight points, discretionary disqualification – and the soft options of the fixed penalty system do not apply.

Furthermore, 'using' a car means more than merely driving it. You 'use' your car even if you merely have it parked on the road outside your house with no immediate intention of driving it. Provided it is still capable of being driven, and so comes within the legal definition of a 'motor vehicle', you breach Section 143 if, for instance, you have let its insurance lapse.

Every policy must be read carefully for its own detailed cover, including whether it is only limited to 'a named driver' or applies to *any* qualified driver; but three main types of motor insurance are available.

Third Party Only

This is the legal minimum cover. It is also the cheapest, although – as with all insurance – the premium will depend on individual circumstances. A seventeen-year-old driver in Rugby, Warwickshire, found this out to his cost in September 2000 when, after buying a Ford Orion Ghia with a £900 inheritance, he was quoted £19,600 for third party insurance! As to the cover, if you have an accident that is partly or even wholly your fault, your insurance company will pay for damage to the vehicle or property of, or bodily injury to, anyone else involved (i.e. the 'third party') – which can include your own passenger. But you will have to pay for repairing or replacing your own car and, if the third party were to blame, your insurers will not help you pursue your claim against him. It is nothing to do with them.

Third Party Fire and Theft

This is one step more than the minimum. It will also cover you against your own car being stolen or damaged in a fire. But no more.

Comprehensive

This is the most expensive form of insurance cover and goes well beyond the legal minimum. It will cover you not only against damage or bodily injury to 'third parties' but also for loss of or damage to your own car up to its insured value.

But, and I only discovered this the hard way after an accident which was not my fault and in which I was nearly killed, it will only cover you against the death or bodily injury of yourself or your spouse travelling with you, and nothing else.

What happens if you are driving someone else's car or they are driving yours?

Many motorists are unclear about this but the law is specific: anyone driving a motor vehicle must be insured to drive that vehicle, either under their own policy or the vehicle owner's policy. If you are 'comprehensively' covered, you will usually be insured to drive someone else's car with their consent – but only for 'third party only' cover, not for injury to yourself! Whatever your own insurance, you should always check that your use of another car is covered, preferably 'comprehensively', by its owner's own policy.

Similarly, if letting someone else drive your car, you should make sure he is insured to drive it. If not, you are at risk of being prosecuted for 'permitting' him to use the car while uninsured – which carries the same heavy penalties as if you were using it yourself without insurance.

NOTE: The Press Office of the Association of British Insurers will, on request, supply free leaflets on car insurance and, in fact, on insurance generally (see **Useful Addresses**).

J

JAIL

When can an ordinary, law-abiding motorist find himself going to jail for a driving offence? Even the best driver can find himself in this dire situation, so it is a question of practical interest to thousands of motorists.

There are two main categories of offence involved: causing death on the roads and drink-driving. No one will be surprised at the first category but, of course, it is not every death on the roads that will lead to a prison sentence – or even the legal possibility of one. As we have seen under **Death on the Roads**, a driver involved in a fatal road accident only faces imprisonment if convicted of manslaughter, causing death by dangerous driving or careless driving while under the influence of drink or drugs, with excess alcohol in the body or having unjustifiably refused a breath test.

Sentences usually range from from three months to seven years, although the possible legal maximum is ten years, and will of course vary enormously depending on the circumstances – and the judge – as the following examples show.

A fifty-four-year-old retired millionaire businessman who killed two pensioners when he crashed into their car while showing off his wife's £130,000 Ferrari at high speed was jailed for nine months and banned from driving for seven years.

A 24-year-old driver convicted in 1998 of causing the death through dangerous driving of two youngsters after his BMW hit a roundabout barrier at 70 mph did not go to jail after being found guilty at the Old Bailey, although he admitted having drunk three pints of lager before the crash. Judge Henry Pownall, QC, merely imposed a five-year driving ban and two 240-hour community orders (to run concurrently).

Another twenty-four-year-old driver speeding at 70 mph in a 30-mph zone in Liverpool's Wavertree area because he was late picking up his parents was talking on a mobile phone and overtaking when he hit a seventy-nine-year-old pedestrian who was hurled into the air and later died from his injuries. The motorist, who had initially lied to the police about using his mobile phone and had only recently completed a three-month ban for careless driving, pleaded guilty at Liverpool Crown Court to causing death by dangerous driving. In August 2000, Judge David Clarke, QC, the Recorder of Liverpool, sent him to jail for three years and imposed a new driving ban of three years to start from the time of his release.

A bad case of drink-driving, even without anyone having been killed, can lead to a jail sentence of up to six months and/or a maximum £5,000 fine and an extended driving ban. For instance, in March 1998, Bury magistrates jailed a thirty-five-year-old woman for two months for driving while four times over the alcohol limit with her ten-year-old daughter in the passenger seat; and two days earlier Horsham magistrates jailed for four months an alcoholic who drove while eight times over the limit. Asked by a police officer how much he had drunk, he had replied, 'Nothing, I have just got back from a detox clinic.' Sadly, it was not true.

Four other offences carry the theoretical possibility of a jail sentence: failing to provide a breath specimen; failing to stop after an accident; failing to report an accident; and driving when disqualified. But in practice a prison term is rare. In the 1993 case of *R*. v. *Cox*, Lord Taylor, then Lord Chief Justice, made clear that a prison sentence should be passed only 'when right-thinking members of the public, knowing all the facts, would feel that justice had not been done by the passing of any other sentence'.

Normally law-abiding motorists are not easily sent to jail.

JOYRIDING

Not a joy for car owners – or for those who think they can get away with 'borrowing' someone else's vehicle (including a bicycle) without the owner's permission and going off on a 'joyride' with impunity. In fact, if caught, they cannot be convicted of stealing because they have not had the intention of depriving the owner of his property (an essential element of the crime of theft) but they are still guilty of the lesser offence of 'taking a vehicle without the owner's consent'. Under Section 12 of the 1968 Theft Act, they can be jailed for up to six months and/or fined up to

£5,000 for a motor vehicle and up to £1,500 for a bicycle. Any passenger is equally guilty and faces similar punishment if they knew the vehicle (or bicycle) had been taken without the owner's consent.

It is no defence that the 'borrower' intended to return it or simply abandoned it. But it is a defence to prove that it was taken in the genuine and reasonable belief that, knowing the circumstances, the owner would have given consent. Magistrates are not fools, however. Such a defence is unlikely to succeed if the defendant was uninsured or without a valid driving licence (as often happens) because, in those circumstances, the owner would also have been committing a criminal offence.

Back in April 1992, in an attempt to stem the rising tide of dangerous and often lethal joyriding on rundown council estates and in other parts of the country, Parliament passed the inelegantly entitled Aggravated Vehicle-taking Act. Now incorporated into the 1968 Theft Act as Section 12A, this states that anyone who unlawfully takes a vehicle and drives it dangerously or causes injury or damage to property on a road or public place, commits the more serious offence of 'aggravated vehicle-taking'. He must be tried in a Crown Court, not a magistrates' court, and faces up to two years in jail and disqualification from driving for at least twelve months. Passengers who know that the vehicle has been taken without the owner's consent are also guilty and, if someone is killed because of the joyrider's driving, the maximum prison sentence goes up to five years. I have always thought that 'joyriding' is a most inappropriate term for this clearly illegal form of driving.

K

KEEPING YOUR JOB

In the summer of 2000 there was the tragic case of a Hertfordshire policeman who hanged himself after being forced to resign following being banned from driving for eighteen months and fined £500 for drink-driving. In the previous four years, six other banned Hertfordshire police officers had been given reprimands, cautions or fines by a police disciplinary panel. Yet this officer, unfortunately involved in an off-duty car accident when returning from a colleague's wedding, was given no such softer option.

Without going into the specific facts of his case – his widow is said to be considering suing the Hertfordshire Constabulary – it raises the fundamental question: when can a drink-driving conviction and the almost inevitable driving ban of at least a year legitimately cost you your job?

If you have worked for the same boss for less than a year, you cannot complain anyway. You can only claim compensation for unfair dismissal if you have been continuously employed by the same employer for at least a year, although not necessarily doing the same work all that time.

But after a year's service, you have certain built-in rights. You cannot be dismissed out of hand simply because driving is part of your job and you cannot drive while banned. Your boss will have to consider very carefully all the relevant circumstances before deciding whether to sack you: otherwise you will be able to take him to your local employment tribunal and claim substantial compensation for unfair dismissal.

The tribunal's decision would depend on many factors: the exact nature of your job, your record in the job, the precise circumstances of the incident that led to the ban, whether you were on or off duty at the time, how the conviction will affect people with whom you must come into contact in connection with your work, etc., etc.

All this can be summed up in the basic proposition that an employer must deal reasonably with the situation: both from his point of view and yours. He must, in effect, perform a balancing act.

That is why, in another case, an off-duty traffic sergeant who failed a breath test at his Dorset police station after returning a police car and was banned for sixteen months and fined £450, was put on non-operational duties and agreed to attend a drink-drive rehabilitation course while he faced an internal inquiry. Nothing is automatic in these cases. As a general rule, as in this Dorset case, if an employee with a good record can be found something else to do, even though driving is normally part of his job, he must be offered such alternative employment. He cannot simply be sacked out of hand.

On the other hand, if the circumstances of the conviction are, in themselves, so reprehensible that it will have an adverse effect upon the employer's business or the employee's ability to perform other functions within the organization, an unfair dismissal claim will not succeed.

This happened, for instance, in the case of a branch manager of a firm of estate agents who admitted to his district manager that he intended pleading guilty to a charge of gross indecency in the local magistrates' court. He lost his job, and the Employment Appeal Tribunal ruled that he had not been dismissed unfairly. The district manager was entitled to consider the effect on his work colleagues and the adverse publicity it would bring to the firm. Relocating him in the office was not a practicable option.

NOTE: Motorists used to be able to obtain insurance entitling them to a chauffeur if they lost their licence for drink-driving, and that could sometimes help them keep their job. But nearly ten years ago the two companies offering such policies withdrew them. It was considered that in some way they encouraged drivers to risk drinking. This type of insurance policy remains on the market – but only for drivers who lose their licences for comparatively short periods for speeding or 'totting up' through accumulating more than twelve penalty points in three years.

KEY IN THE IGNITION

Can leaving your key in the ignition – even for just a few minutes – invalidate your insurance if a thief jumps into your vehicle and drives away?

That was my opening question in a 'Street Legal' in 1997. I was commenting on a case where a motorist from Weybridge had pulled into a filling station in Ewell,

Surrey, dashed in to buy a snack, leaving the key in the ignition, and emerged less than a minute later to find that someone had driven off with his £12,500 BMW. His AA-linked insurance company refused to pay on the basis that his policy contained the usual clause that you must take 'all reasonable steps' to safeguard your vehicle, and the AA was unable to help.

My comment was that, on the law as it then stood, the company was within its legal rights and, as I wrote, 'except in an emergency or (possibly) in a remote spot with no one else around, a motorist who leaves his car's keys in the ignition has only himself to blame if it is stolen'. But in a 'Street Legal' in November 1999, nearly two years later, I discussed a new High Court ruling, in *Hayward* v. *Norwich Union*, that substantially changed the law.

What happened was that Mr Hayward, driving his almost new £65,000 Porsche from his office in Cardiff to London along the A48, turned off at a petrol station near Newport to fill up with petrol for the journey. As usual with a luxury car of that type, it was controlled by an immobilizer which came on automatically thirty seconds after the engine had been turned off. After filling up with petrol, Mr Hayward slipped the immobilizer under his seat where it could not be seen and went into a nearby kiosk to pay – leaving the key in the ignition.

He was standing in a queue waiting to pay, with the car in his vision all the time, when he heard the noise of its engine. He promptly ran out and found a man sitting in the driving seat. He could see the man's hands 'fiddling with a box' on his lap – later assumed to be a device used by professional thieves to override high-performance cars' immobilizers – before the engine revved very loudly and he had to jump out of the way as the car sped off. The whole incident took less than thirty seconds.

Norwich Union refused to honour Mr Hayward's £66,650 claim (the value of the car plus £1,550 for a computer and a coat left inside) on the basis that he was in breach of two conditions in his policy. These are found in most motor insurance policies and exempt companies from paying out for 'loss or damage from theft whilst the ignition keys of your car have been left in or on the car' and also state: 'You shall at all times take all reasonable steps to safeguard your car from loss or damage.'

On 22 October 1999, Deputy High Court Judge Michael Tugendhat, QC, ruled that, despite the policy's clear wording and the undoubted fact that Mr Hayward had left the key in the ignition (mistakenly thinking that the immobilizer could not be overridden), he had none the less acted reasonably in all the circumstances and had not been reckless. The Deputy Judge based his decision on a 1967 ruling by Lord Justice Diplock in *Fraser* v. *Furman Productions Ltd*, a case involving employers' liability insurance towards their staff, and, for the first time, applied it to motor insurance. He quoted with approval this dictum by Sir Kenneth Diplock, who later became a Law Lord: 'It is not enough that the employer's omission to take any particular precautions to avoid accidents should be negligent; it must be at least reckless, that is to say, made with actual recognition by the insured himself that a danger exists, and not caring whether or not it is averted. The purpose of the condition is to ensure that the insured will not, because he is covered against loss by the policy, refrain from taking precautions which he knows ought to be taken.'

In other words, although most motor insurance policies say expressly that drivers 'must be reasonable', the courts are entitled to rewrite that to mean 'must not be reckless'. It is little surprise that almost immediately Norwich Union announced that it would appeal against Deputy Judge Tugendhat's ruling.

Perhaps of even more interest for the motoring public than the ruling itself is the unique insight that Tugendhat's judgment gave into the way that the motor insurance industry itself treats this situation. For it quoted two internal memoranda by Norwich Union's Motor Claims Manager, dating back to 1995 and 1996, that would otherwise never have seen the light of day.

In the earlier one, the Claims Manager said, 'It is not always appropriate to interpret the keys exception on a literal basis, for example we would not be looking to decline the claim whereby the policy holder had essentially been "hijacked" due to him being in the vehicle *or standing adjacent to the same* [my italics], albeit that the keys may be in the ignition.'

In the later memorandum, dealing with 'reasonable care', he was even more forthcoming: 'This is a very difficult area on which to provide general advice as all claims have to be considered on their merit. However, we would expect Claims Handlers to adopt a realistic approach before deciding to invoke this policy condition. *The Courts will only support us with a repudiation if there has been a reckless disregard by the insured for the security of their property and the Insurance Ombudsman has confirmed they will adopt this similar interpretation* [again, my italics].'

My own insurance broker, 'fascinated' by these two statements, tells me that they confirm his own recent experience with several companies. 'Ten years ago, there would have been no discretion. Nowadays there is,' he says. In February 2001, the case finally reached the Appeal Court and Deputy Judge Tugenhadt QC's ruling was overturned. So a saga that began three years earlier, in February 1998, with the original theft of Mr Hayward's car ended with his having to hand back his payout to the insurance company. Few motorists will be entirely surprised.

KILLING WHILE CARELESS

In January 1999, the important Appeal Court decision of *R.* v. *Simmonds* only appeared in the specialized Road Traffic Reports of leading cases but it deserves to be far better known. It relates to the proper penalty for a court to impose if a motorist is guilty of careless driving which, without any element of drink-driving, has killed someone.

None of us is perfect. Any of us, at any given moment, can be capable of an error of judgement at the wheel of a motor vehicle which would amount, in law, to careless driving.

It is the lowest level of driving offence and, if a driver is convicted, the penalties laid down by the 1988 Road Traffic

Act reflect that comparative lack of severity. They are a maximum fine of £2,500 (but usually only about £200 is imposed for a first offence where no one has been injured), endorsement with three to nine penalty points and – rarely – disqualification which, when it is imposed, is usually only for a year.

But what if careless driving, without any suggestion of improper alcohol intake, kills someone – as it easily can? What then are the likely penalties?

Under no circumstances can they can be more than the maxima laid down by the Act. The tragic circumstance that someone has died does not, of itself, notch up the severity of the offence. The only way in which one could be jailed for careless driving, even though causing the death of an innocent human being, is, as we have seen earlier under **Death on the Roads**, if the driver is under the influence of drink or drugs, has excess alcohol in the body or has unjustifiably refused to take a breath test.

Then there can be an unlimited fine and/or up to ten years in prison, with Appeal Court decisions indicating that the average jail term should be around five years.

But so long as the actual badness of the driving does not rise above the level of carelessness, the penalty, even within the framework of a £2,500 maximum fine, rare disqualification and the rest, has – until January 1999 – not been likely to be increased because it has caused death. As Lord Lane, then Lord Chief Justice, laid down in *R.* v. *Krawec* in 1985, 'In our judgment the unforeseen and unexpected results of the carelessness are not in themselves relevant to penalty.'

This decision was understandably popular with motorists but not with those mourning the death of a loved one. I give just two examples.

A thirty-seven-year-old man lost control of his car when travelling at high speed over a humpback bridge in Cleveland. He collided head-on with an oncoming vehicle, killing its driver and his own two young women passengers. In January 1996, Teesside magistrates fined him £1,500 and banned him from driving for six months. The victims' relatives gasped and shouted their disbelief as the punishment was announced.

In November 1998, a driver who pleaded guilty to careless driving had jumped a red light and ploughed into a family on a pedestrian crossing, killing a child in a pushchair. But Exeter magistrates only fined him £200, banned him from driving for three years and ordered him to pay £35 costs. Not surprisingly, the child's mother condemned the 'obscenity' of what she described as 'trivial' punishment .

But it is unlikely to happen again. For Lord Justice Henry, giving judgment in *R. v. Simmonds* for two other appeal judges and himself, ruled that Lord Lane's earlier ruling was no longer appropriate. He said that the law had moved on and in 1991 Parliament had created the two new offences of causing death by dangerous driving and causing death by careless driving while under the influence of drink or drugs or with excess alcohol in the body, etc.

He therefore felt able to lay down a new guideline for magistrates: 'In the current context of a statutory regime for road traffic offences that envisages the causing of death as a factor leading to an enhanced statutory sentencing bracket, the courts regard additional deaths as an aggravating factor and we find the concept of a road traffic offence in which the sentencing court is obliged to disregard the fact that a death has been caused as wholly anomalous.'

The message is clear: drivers whose carelessness causes death are still not at risk of going to jail but henceforth they face fines and penalty points much closer to the maximum, plus more frequent, and probably much longer, disqualification. In its revised edition of *Sentencing Guidelines for Magistrates*, published in September 2000, the Magistrates' Association advised its members to heed the message contained in Lord Justice Henry's judgment. What many have seen as the old licence to kill has gone – and not before time.

L

LACED DRINKS

Can you save your licence after drink-driving if your drink was laced without your knowledge? Some people have the strangest sense of humour and think it amusing to 'spike' a motorist's drink. The judges have ruled that if the unwitting driver is then found guilty of drink-driving and the spiked part of his drink was enough to push him over the legal limit which otherwise would not have been the case (this is essential), he stands a chance of not losing his licence for the usually inevitable minimum of twelve months.

The first major High Court ruling dates back to February 1973. It was in the case of *Pugsley* v. *Hunter*. One evening a motorist had consumed (so he thought) two light ales and a shandy in a south-east London public house. While he was in the lavatory before getting back into his car, a so-called friend had added two double vodkas to his drink. When he was stopped by the police, his blood was found to contain 161 mg of alcohol in 100 ml of blood – just over twice the legal limit.

A London stipendiary magistrate said there were 'special reasons' that allowed him to exercise his discretion to let the man keep his licence, and on appeal the High

Court upheld this basic principle. Even so, the Lord Chief Justice, then Lord Widgery, commented wryly, 'This is a defence not uncommon at the present time ... it is a defence no doubt which magistrates will examine with some care.'

Those words have been heeded. The courts do not fall over themselves to uphold the 'laced-drink defence', as lawyers cynically call it. The possibilities for abuse are evident and everyone knows that the best way not to be guilty of drink-driving is not to drink at all before driving. So making the laced-drink defence succeed in court is (quite rightly) something of an obstacle course.

The motorist must show that there has been an intervention by a third party which has misled him, as when a pub landlord advised his customer that a brand of diabetic lager was weaker than ordinary lager when it was, in fact, twice as strong. Or when a barman muddled up his beer taps and pulled a stronger beer than the one ordered.

It is not enough for a driver to think he can safely 'ration' his drink. As the High Court ruled in 1974, 'A person who combines drinking with driving has a very heavy responsibility.'

It is up to the driver to prove, if necessary by medical evidence, that he would not have been over the limit without the spiked part of his drink, although as Lord Widgery acknowledged, 'there are some cases where it can be obvious that the added drink was the cause of the offence. An example is where the alcoholic content in the blood is only marginally over the statutory limit and the added drink is substantial.'

A motorist also has to prove that he was not at fault in failing to realize that he was not in a fit state to drive. The High Court re-emphasized this in *Donahue* v. *DPP*, where magistrates found that 'special reasons' existed – but still chose to disqualify. What happened was that a motorist attending a company function asked for non-alcoholic wine but was served alcoholic wine. Immediately after he drove away, his car left the road. He had a blood alcohol content of 99 µg of alcohol to 100 ml of breath (the legal limit is 35 µg).

Local magistrates agreed that 'special reasons' existed, but said that even so, the motorist must have realised he was unfit to drive – they refused to exercise their discretion not to disqualify. On appeal, his counsel argued that the two findings were inconsistent: a Bench could not say that 'special reasons' existed and still disqualify. But the High Court said that the magistrates had considered all relevant matters properly and had not erred in the exercise of their discretion.

The law of drink-driving is strongly enforced and defences, even when legitimate, are strictly contained.

LAWNMOWER

This is perhaps a surprising entry in a book on motoring law but there was in 1987 a classic case, reported anonymously in the *Solicitors' Journal* for lawyers' enlightenment, of a woman who had had too much to drink and was found driving a lawnmower on a road. She was breath-tested, found over the limit and prosecuted for drink-driving and driving while disqualified and without insurance.

The contraption was undoubtedly being driven along a road (a cul-de-sac, in fact, but that made no legal differ-ence) and she did not deny that she was over the limit – but she would only have been guilty of the offences if the lawnmower was, in law, a 'motor vehicle' within the meaning of the 1972 Road Traffic Act: i.e. a mechanically propelled vehicle intended or adapted for use on roads. The same definition is now contained in the 1988 version of the same Act.

Some mowing machines – for instance, those used on the grass verges of roads – are legally motor vehicles and one has to pass a driving test to drive them. But this machine was only intended to be used in country gardens and caravan parks. It was, in fact, a Westwood Laser L18 garden tractor with an 11-hp rotary Honda engine, and had been driven over to a party. Later the woman in question, a little the worse for wear, had clambered on board and driven it some 50 yards along the cul-de-sac – where a policeman appeared, and she was breath-tested and arrested. The contraption had a rotary cutting deck fitted underneath and was just over 5 feet long. It had five forward gears and one reverse gear, and the engine had to be stopped to change gear because the gear to be used depended on the kind of grass-cutting operation being undertaken. It had two ornamental front lights but no rear lights, stop lights or indicators, and a representative of the manufacturers told the local magistrates' court that it had not been intended or adapted for use on a road. However, the police grimly contended that the manufacturers may not have intended it to be used on a road – but the woman defendant certainly did!

What happened? The magistrates used their common sense and acquitted her of all charges with her legal costs ordered to be paid out of public funds. The rest of the story was even more farcical. Using taxpayers' money, the Crown Prosecution Service tried to appeal to the High Court but there was delay, and the High Court refused to hear the case out of time. Much public money had been spent but at least, as the *Solicitors' Journal* tartly observed, 'The case is of some importance as to the nature in law of a motor vehicle.'

LEARNER DRIVERS

We have already seen, under **Driving Test**, that no learner is allowed out on a road or other public place – as against private land – without being accompanied by someone aged at least twenty-one who has held a full British licence for that type of car for at least three years. Furthermore, as Mr Justice Hilbery laid down as far back as 1940, 'It is [that person's] duty, when necessary, to do whatever can reasonably be expected to prevent the driver from acting unskilfully or carelessly or in a manner likely to cause danger to others.'

But there has even been a case in which that duty was extended to include an official examiner taking a learner out on his driving test. It was in October 1980 when Judge Henry Kershaw ruled at Barnsley Crown Court that a thirty-nine-year-old examiner had rightly been convicted of aiding and abetting a driving-test candidate to drive without due care and attention – while taking his driving test! A nineteen-year-old learner had misunderstood the examiner's instructions and turned into a one-way street the wrong way but the examiner had said nothing – until they crashed into another car.

Judge Kershaw said, 'While examiners are not in the same category as supervisors or instructors, neither are they merely passengers. If a candidate is so incompetent that to continue the test would be a serious danger to the public, the examiner must terminate it.'

Similar considerations apply to the question of civil liability. Other road users must be protected. The standard of driving on the roads has to be objective. A learner's inexperience is no excuse if his negligent driving causes an accident. As Lord Denning once said, with typical bluntness, 'The standard of driving must be that of a reasonable motorist not that of a reasonable learner motorist.' Furthermore, if the accident could have been averted by the accompanying driver using reasonable supervision, he – or his insurance company – will have to share the cost of compensation.

LEGAL LOOPHOLES

These mainly occur in drink-driving cases but they are nothing like so prevalent – or humorous – as in the early days when suspected drink-driving motorists offered their penis for a blood-test hypodermic syringe or barrack-room lawyers carried a hip-flask of whisky in their back-pocket so as to have a quick swig before the police could take a breath test.

Nowadays loopholes are few and far between – but they can still be found, as in a case in July 1997 when a motorist, asked if there were any medical reasons why blood should not be taken from him, replied that he did not like needles. He refused to give blood and was convicted of failing to provide a specimen 'without legal excuse'. The High Court quashed the conviction on appeal. Mr Justice Buxton ruled that the constable's question was too limited. He should not have asked whether there was any medical reason for not taking blood but whether there was 'any' reason. A motorist can have a legitimate excuse that is not a medical excuse. How's that for lateral thinking?

Few people are at their best at 2.37 a.m., least of all when they have been stopped driving, positively breath-alysed, arrested, taken to a police station – and put through the standard police procedure for establishing the exact amount of alcohol in their breath.

This certainly applied to a worried motorist standing in the police station in Easby, North Yorkshire, having just been told that he had 47 µg of alcohol in 100 ml of his breath (the legal limit is 35 μg). 'So what happens now?' he must have asked himself. The answer was that the police sergeant told him that because the specimen showed less than 50 μg, the 1998 Road Traffic Act allowed him to have it replaced by a blood or urine sample, which would then be sent for laboratory analysis.

A vital exchange of words then followed.

Sergeant: 'The specimen requested can be either blood or urine. This is decided by the police officer. In this instance the specimen I require will be blood. Have you any objection to this?'

Motorist: 'No.'

A police doctor was called and a blood sample taken. That was nearly an hour later – but the motorist still had 90 μg of alcohol in 100 ml of his blood (the legal limit is 80 μg). So, not surprisingly, he ended up in a local magistrates' court charged with driving with excess alcohol in his blood – but he was acquitted. The prosecution appealed, and the High Court in London upheld the acquittal. So there was no disqualification, no fine, nothing. How come?

The answer is that, because the judges have evolved the doctrine that, when a motorist is given the choice of blood or urine at the police station (either because his breath registers '50–100' or else because no breath-testing device is available), the choice is not his but that of the police officer. But the policeman must ask the motorist for his views – which this Yorkshire police sergeant did not. He told the motorist it was going to be blood, and that was it.

As Lord Justice (now Lord) Bingham ruled: 'It is for the

police officer to make the decision whether the sample shall be blood or urine but he must give the defendant an opportunity to consider which sample he would prefer and any reasons for that preference. Thus, when the police officer comes to make his decision he must do so knowing of the defendant's preference and any reason the defendant may have given for it. He must not address the defendant in terms which suggest that the sample *must* [my italics] be of one rather than the other and until the two possibilities have been explained to him and a fair opportunity given to say, if he wishes, which he would prefer to give and why.'

In subsequent cases the High Court has on several occasions used this ruling to quash alleged drink-driving motorists' convictions, which may seem somewhat strange. But the police have brought this on themselves. Too many station sergeants still do not say something simple like: 'You can now give a sample of blood or urine. The ultimate decision is mine but I will listen to whatever you have to say.' They prefer to use stultifying police jargon rather than simple English.

As a matter of policy, the police prefer blood samples because, as Lord Justice Watkins has said, 'Taking samples of urine is a messy business.' But they must still give the motorist a chance to express his own views. What is doubly ironic is that, in their own best interests, motorists should choose blood anyway because the delay in getting the police doctor to the station to take the sample will help the alcohol to disappear from their blood.

M

METERS

What is the law on parking at an out-of-order meter? The question is simple but, as so often in motoring law, the answer is not. It all depends on the type of meter.

Let us consider first the old-fashioned mechanical meter that still prevails in many cities and towns outside central London. Many motorists – and even traffic wardens and parking attendants – believe it is an offence to park in a bay where the meter has been officially bagged by a warden or where, without such a 'No Parking' bag, the meter is out of order.

In fact, the law is unclear and it is possible to argue that no offence is committed here. This arises from the unsatisfactory case of *Wilson* v. *Arnott*, in which the High Court ruled in November 1976, on appeal from Luton magistrates, that an officially suspended parking bay still remained a 'designated parking place', within the meaning of a local 'No Waiting' order. So, unless a motorist was loading or unloading goods, he automatically committed an offence by parking there – even though, with the best will in the world, he could not pay by putting coins in a bagged meter! What makes the problem worse is that not one of the three appeal judges gave any guidance about the legal position if the meter was unusable not because it was bagged but simply because it was out of order.

As *Butterworths' Road Traffic Service*, a leading legal textbook, rightly says, 'It would have been interesting if the court had been required to consider the guilt of a well-intentioned driver who parked in the bay in the expectation of paying the local authority charge, whilst being prevented from doing so by the local authority providing a parking meter which was out of order. The local authority has a duty to provide meters and apparatus. Clearly, there is ground to be explored.'

Sadly, that has not happened and the law remains uncertain. However, it may help readers to know that I once successfully used Butterworths' argument to persuade a local authority with an old-style meter to withdraw its fixed-penalty charge.

But this argument cannot possibly prevail with the new-style electronic meters which show the parking time purchased on a digital display. These were first introduced by Westminster City Council and have now spread through most of central London and into an increasing number of other major cities. Here the law is, sadly, entirely clear – and deadly to the motorist. These meters conform to a standard design and generally bear a metal plate stating bluntly: 'No parking at an out-of-order meter'. In addition, most, if not all, local 'No Waiting' orders where electronic meters have been installed make 'parking in an out-of-order meter bay during controlled hours' a specific offence. 'It is for the benefit of all law-abiding drivers,' a Westminster official has told me. 'Unscrupulous motorists used to jam meters with foreign coins or otherwise vandalize them so they could claim they were out of order. Now, far fewer meters are tampered with and more are available to the law-abiding public.'

The AA is not so sure. It says the new-style meters are not infallible and that cases have occurred where meters wrongly display 'out of order' before parking time has expired, and some over-zealous parking attendants are authorizing clamping or removing vehicles parked when the meter is still functioning correctly. Yet all is not grim. The Parking Committee for London, responsible for supervising the capital's parking laws, says in its helpful pamphlet, *Paying to Park*, 'If a meter with no "out-of-order" sign takes your money and fails to register the time, do not attempt to put more coins in: place a note on the windscreen saying "Meter out of order – wouldn't take change", with the date and time you parked, and leave the car where it is.' But it adds: 'The meter will then be checked – and if there is no fault, you will get a parking ticket.' After all, not every motorist is a saint.

MOPEDS AND MOTORCYCLES

What is the legal difference between these vehicles?

A moped is a less powerful type of motorcycle and is a motor vehicle of not more than 50 cc with a maximum speed of 30 mph. To ride one, you must be sixteen or over, begin with a provisional moped licence and complete Compulsory Basic Training (CBT) (see **Driving Test**).

A moped is legally a kind of motorcycle but the latter is a more embracing term. It is more powerful and can even include a three-wheeler car. It is, according to Section 185 of the 1988 Road Traffic Act, a motor vehicle – but not an invalid carriage – with fewer than four wheels that weighs less than 410 kg (920 lb) when unladen. To ride one, you must be seventeen or over, and the type of licence with which you must start will depend on its cubic capacity, but, as with mopeds, you will also have had to complete CBT.

For mopeds there is no minimum depth of tyre tread, although there must be visible tread across the breadth and around the tyre's entire circumference. Motorcycles must have at least 1 mm depth of tread throughout a continuous band measuring at least three-quarters of the breadth of the tread, and around the tyre's entire outer circumference.

A pillion passenger cannot be carried on either a moped or a motorcycle until the rider has a full moped or motorcycle licence. Except with a motorcycle which has a sidecar, the rider cannot carry more than one passenger, who must sit astride a fixed pillion seat.

All riders and their pillion passengers on both mopeds and motorcycles, except Sikhs wearing turbans, must wear crash helmets approved by the British Safety Standards Institute with the chin strap worn according to the manufacturer's instructions. Not wearing a helmet while travelling is an offence with a maximum £500 fine and can lead to your compensation being reduced if you are injured in an accident.

MOT

A few weeks ago I took my car in for its first MoT and it passed the test with flying colours. The examiner gave me my test certificate without a single adverse comment. Yet within days I had a flat tyre and when I took it in to be replaced, the fitter said that my alignment was also in a dangerous condition and needed to be corrected. 'That's not possible,' I protested. 'I've just had the car MoT-ed! The examiner should have tested the steering!' But the fitter was unimpressed and still insisted that the job needed to be done.

Of course, I agreed but I began to wonder just what is the value of an MoT test certificate. Hence this entry.

For a start, I, of all people, should have read the small print on the back of the certificate. In fact, it is quite specific: 'This certificate confirms that the vehicle described over the page was examined according to Section 45 of the Road Traffic Act 1988 and met the standards required by law. However, [it] only confirms that the vehicle met the minimum acceptable standards at the time it was tested.'

As an AA spokesman comments, 'Our main concern about the MoT test is that it basically gives a snapshot of the condition of the car on one particular day and at that particular moment. You could have driven the car away afterwards and clipped the kerb, and that would have made it immediately "unroadworthy". Or an indicator bulb could have gone within five seconds of leaving the test and you could have been pulled over by the police.'

Ted Craker, an experienced London vehicle examiner, highlights another shortcoming: 'Checking the steering does not include checking the alignment. They are two separate matters.'

A West London car dealer is even more scathing: 'Test certificates are not worth the paper they're written on!' Not for the first time, and not only in connection with motor-vehicles, the law is at variance with fact.

So let us go back to basic principles.

It is an offence for anyone, whether a motor trader or a private individual, to sell a motor vehicle 'in an unroad-worthy condition', and anyone who uses one in a *dangerous* condition on a road commits an offence against Section 40A of the 1988 Road Traffic Act. The sentence is a maximum £2,500 fine, endorsement with three points and discretion-ary disqualification.

Few people use cars that are positively 'dangerous' but many drivers may occasionally be in breach of the 1986 Motor Vehicle (Construction and Use) Regulations. These create a whole range of maintenance offences, varying from inefficient brakes to having no water in a windscreen-washer bottle.

According to Section 45 of the 1988 Act, the test certifi-cate is supposed to ensure that the 1986 Regulations are complied with and that the vehicle's use on a road 'would not involve a danger of injury to any person'. It was first introduced back in the Fifties for cars more than ten years old. But the age limit was progressively reduced and the Act now makes it an offence to use on a road any car older than three years without a current certificate.

The certificate lasts for a year and, if you are caught without a current one, you can be fined up to £1,000. It is no good saying, 'I am just taking in the car for its test, officer.' Under the 1981 Motor Vehicles (Tests) Regulations, that is only a defence if you are taking it in 'by previous arrangement'. Those words mean what they say. Sometimes defendants argue that they have not made a specific appointment but are on their way to a testing-station garage which advises that tests can be given without prior notice. That is not good enough. Many magistrates' courts convict on the basis that 'previous arrangement' means that the car owner must have specifically contacted the testing station beforehand to arrange the test.

The 1981 Regulations specify what examiners must test. It is a long list including brakes, steering, lighting equipment, reflectors, stop lights, tyres, seat-belts, direction indicators, windscreen wipers and washers, exhaust system, audible warning instrument, bodywork and suspension.

That, at least, is the theory but, in the words of a helpful AA spokesman, 'There are quite a range of inconsistencies. You can take a vehicle for a test and get a different series of findings if you took it to another garage. You have to expect that, where there is a certain amount of human interpretation, you are going to get some variation. The system is not ideal but it does a pretty good job at keeping the wrecks off the road.'

That may well be true; but on BBC *Breakfast News* there was a feature where an AA engineer examined a reporter's vehicle and highlighted various defects. She then took the car on to various garages where they missed a couple of fairly important items. One was that the wrong bulb had been fitted on one stop light so that it shone less brightly than the stop light on the other side. This was highly dangerous because someone travelling behind in the dark might easily have thought that the vehicle was a motor-cycle not a car.

Undoubtedly, the MoT testing system will be enhanced when, as planned, it will be linked to an electronic database that will enable documentation to be checked and vehicles ferreted out that have previously been written off.

But that will still not alter the basic situation that the test certificate is only a snapshot in time of a car's perform-ance and that it is, like so many other things in life, subject to human error.

MOTOR INSURERS' BUREAU

This Bureau, established in 1946, is funded by the motor insurance companies and provides compensation where the victim of a road accident would otherwise be without remedy. It does so by nominating an insurance company to deal with the victim, as though the motorist responsible for the accident was insured with them. But it is restricted to cases where the person responsible is uninsured or, as in 'hit-and-run' cases, untraced. The amount of compensation is the same as a court would award in similar circumstances. Where the guilty driver is uninsured, there is no limit in claims for death or personal injuries but claims for damage to property are capped at £250,000 with, in both instances, a £175 excess. With 'hit-and-run' cases, where the driver is by the very nature of things untraced, there is no compensation at all for damage to property.

Furthermore, the Bureau will never pay out to a victim of an accident who was driving a vehicle that was uninsured or was being driven in a vehicle that he or she knew or ought to have known was uninsured, stolen, unlawfully taken or driven by an under-age driver (see **Hit and Run**).

MOTOR VEHICLE

We have already seen under **Lawnmower** that nice questions can sometimes arise in court over the precise legal meaning of this term. Another such case was in April 1999 when an eagle-eyed police officer spotted a twenty-eight-year-old Gloucester businessman riding a 20-mph Chinese Scootech electric scooter on a station platform and then out on to a road. The officer stopped him and five months later the man appeared at Gloucester Magistrates' Court charged with driving a 'motor vehicle' without insurance. The defence lawyer argued that the Scootechs were designed to be scooted up hills and the manufacturers had not intended them to be used on roads. 'It has no provision for number plates, indicators, horns, a seat, shock absorbers or springs,' he said. The magistrates were impressed and ruled that the scooter was not a motor vehicle within the meaning of the 1988 Road Traffic Act and its rider did not therefore need to be insured.

One wonders why some cases are ever brought to court.

MOTORWAYS

Most of us know something about the special legal rules that apply to motorways: no learner drivers, tractors, cyclists or moped riders, no picking up or setting down of passengers, etc.

(See also **Queasy or Tired**).

The 'soft option' of a fixed penalty applies to motorway driving offences, but the following two situations may cause problems.

Leaving the motorway

Do not, like so many drivers, suddenly pull off an outside lane in front of drivers in the nearside left-hand lane who then may have to brake sharply. If a police patrol were to see you do this, you could be warned about inconsiderate driving (see **Overtaking**). Similarly, if pulling on to the hard shoulder in an emergency or when directed to do so by official traffic signs or the police, you should, even if already in the left-hand lane, try not to pull abruptly on to the shoulder but first slow down so that traffic behind is not inconvenienced.

Can you lawfully make a U-turn on the motorway to go back the other way and avoid a long traffic jam ahead?

You risk a fine of up to £2,500, endorsement of your licence with three to six penalty points and discretionary disqualification for breach of Regulation 10 of the 1982 Motorways Traffic (England and Wales) Regulations. You could even be charged with careless or dangerous driving. But if you merely take advantage of a convenient gap in the central reservation, *and you are careful*, you may consider it worth the risk. You will still be fined – but you may avoid penalty points.

In a 1988 case where a motorist on the M23 had driven through a gap and started to drive back along the other carriageway after an accident had caused a major traffic jam ahead, the High Court ruled that local magistrates had been right not to endorse his licence. Mr Justice French said, 'If the motorway had been in normal use, it would have been difficult, perhaps impossible, for the justices to have found "special reasons" not to endorse. However, the motorway was plainly not in normal use. The defendant did not have to halt before executing his U-turn. He was already at a halt. He had ample opportunity to study the carriageway into which he was about to turn.'

Those last words are vital. The driver had not cut across oncoming traffic. He had carefully assessed the situation. Nowadays, he might just be offered a fixed penalty – but I doubt it.

MOVING TRAFFIC OFFENCE

Two *Daily Telegraph* readers once wrote to me independently of each other to say that they had been stopped for breath-testing, although neither had committed any 'moving traffic offence' or been involved in an accident. How was this possible when I had written in an earlier 'Street Legal' that either was essential before a uniformed police officer could stop and breathalyse you and that, accordingly, random breath tests were unlawful?

The answer is that they were both examples of random *stopping*, not random testing. Let me explain. Section 163 of the 1988 Road Traffic Act allows a uniformed police constable to stop a motor vehicle at any time on the road without giving any reason or even having one. But that does not mean he can then automatically breath-test the driver. Lord Widgery, when Lord Chief Justice, ruled as far back as 1972 that if the constable then smells alcohol on the driver's breath, he can ask for the test. 'The mere fact that a check can be described as random is no grounds for dismissing a drink-driving charge,' said Lord Widgery.

The logic is impeccable, but random stopping is all too often a device used by zealous police officers to get round the legal embargo on random testing. In particular, it is often used to justify testing of motorists driving away from a country public house when their handling of their car is without blemish. In law, as in life, there is often more than one way of skinning a cat.

MUST

Must parking attendants and traffic wardens give you a
ticket if they see you parking illegally?

'Yes,' the managing director of one of the private contractors responsible for enforcing the law in London once
wrote to me. 'If parking attendants see a parking offence,
they have no choice but to issue a penalty charge notice.'
The parking enforcement manager of a London council
agreed – but with this slight twist: 'Parking attendants are
highly visible public figures who attract a great deal of
public scrutiny. If they are seen to take action against one
vehicle but not others for no apparent reason, then the
public quite rightly are going to ask why . . . Discretion by
parking attendants is a route to inconsistency. If any discretion is subsequently called for, it can be applied at a
later stage by the council.'

'That may seem impressive,' a friend at the AA commented at the time, 'but the London councils have consis-
tently refused to publish their statistics which would
enable the public to see for themselves the circumstances
in which discretion has been exercised.'

Quite so. In any event, why should the onus be on a
motorist to write a letter of complaint to the local council
before he obtains justice? Why should not parking attendants or traffic wardens who have not yet started to write
out their ticket have a discretion – as police officers have
always had – as to whether or not to start the legal process?
Is it perhaps because we cannot trust them to withstand

the corrupting arrogance of power? In fact, the whole 'feel' of English law has always been in favour of discretion. 'Must' is not a word that has found legal favour in this regard. As Sir Hartley (now Lord) Shawcross, QC, famously said, when Attorney General, back in January 1951, 'It has never been the rule in this country – I hope it never will be – that suspected criminal offences must automatically be the subject of prosecution.'

That is still the law of England, whether applied to minor traffic offences or serious crime. The only problem is that when law enforcement for parking offences is put into the hands of local councils who pocket the proceeds, the profit motive rears its ugly head. Justice is one commodity that should never have been privatized.

N

NIGHT DRIVING

Have you ever wondered what the exact legal requirements are about headlamps and sidelights when driving at night?

The 1989 Road Vehicles Lighting Regulations state that 'between sunset and sunrise' you must use headlights and also in daylight 'when visibility is seriously reduced'.

But you must not 'use any lights in a way which would dazzle or cause discomfort to other road users'. Arrogant motorists like driving, by both night and day, with their headlights full on, irrespective of weather and traffic conditions. They use their lights as a weapon to intimidate others into pulling over and letting them pass. They are breaking the law and a policeman could and, in my opinion, *should* stop them. It is every motorist's legal duty to use dipped headlights, or dim-dip if fitted, at night in built-up areas *and* in dull daytime weather. As the Highway Code spells out, drivers should keep their headlights dipped when overtaking until they are level with the other vehicle, when they should change to main beam unless this would dazzle oncoming traffic. And if you are the one who is dazzled, you should slow down and, if necessary, stop.

If you need to warn other road users of your presence at night, you should flash your headlights. And remember: you must not use your horn between 11.30 p.m. and 7.00 a.m. in a built-up area – except to avoid danger from a moving vehicle, yours or someone else's.

NOISE

We all hate music blaring from other cars, but are these selfish drivers breaking the law? Until the summer of 1996, I would not have been sure of the answer to that question. But an imaginative prosecution by the Gwent Constabulary and local Crown Prosecution Service, coupled with a robust decision by the Hawarden magistrates, now enables me to say: 'Yes, an offence is being committed.'

What happened was that the thudding beat of loud pop music pulsating through the North Wales village of Buckley could be heard from 150 yards away. A police constable easily identified the source of the din: a ghetto-blaster slung across the seat of a Vauxhall Astra GTE being driven through the village. He shouted at the driver to turn down the volume, only for him to reply, 'I can't hear you – the music is too loud.' The car sped off but was later spotted by the constable in a nearby car park. Result: the driver was later charged before the Hawarden magistrates with a breach of Regulation 97 of the 1986 Road Vehicles (Construction and Use) Regulations.

But Regulation 97 says nothing about car radios, ghetto-blasters or other forms of music dissemination. It merely says: 'No motor vehicle shall be used on a road in such manner as to cause any excessive noise which could have been avoided by the exercise of reasonable care on the part of the driver.' The penalty is a fine of up to £1,000. As the defendant's solicitor rightly said in court, the Regulation was normally used only to cover excessive noise from car exhausts and horns – not from a ghetto-blaster or other kind of music player that did not form an integral part of the structure of the car.

But the Bench took the pragmatic view that the Regulation's wording was sufficiently wide to cover any type of excessive noise caused by a driver's unreasonable use of a motor vehicle. It did not matter that the source was not a car radio forming part of the equipment of the vehicle. The excessive noise was caused by the use of the car and could have been avoided by reasonable care on the part of the driver – so the magistrates convicted him and fined him £60 with £30 costs.

As perhaps might have been expected, the driver then complained: 'The police should be out catching burglars and muggers instead of worrying about the volume of my radio.' He also said that he planned to appeal but he never did. So the Hawarden decision stood as a precedent for other magistrates, and over the intervening years there have been several successful prosecutions. One of the worst cases was in 1997 when eleven drivers were fined a total of almost £4,000 after they had played dance music on their car stereos into the early hours of the morning on the sea front in Weston-super-Mare, Somerset. Some of the cars had up to eight speakers and two amplifiers. Some people find pleasure in the strangest ways.

This case was followed up in September 2000 when a motorist waiting at a level crossing in his home town of Worthing, West Sussex, with his car windows open, was fined £20 on the spot for playing loud music. The police officer followed the driver for about a mile and told him he could hear the bass while travelling 30 yards behind him (see **Fixed Penalty System**).

NUMBER PLATES

Technically, these are what the law calls 'registration marks' and each motor vehicle, when first registered, is given such a 'mark' which, according to the 1971 Road Vehicles (Registration and Licensing) Regulations, has to be placed on a metal plate at the front and back of the vehicle. To show you the complexity – and, at times, the stupidity – of the law I cannot resist quoting the following from the current (nineteenth) edition of *Wilkinson's Road Traffic Offences*.

'Regulations 17–22 of, and Schedules 2 and 3 to, the 1971 Regulations relate to the exhibition and position of registration marks; for vehicles first registered before 1 January 1973 the figures and letters must be white, silver or light grey, indelible and on a black surface, save where translucent; or where the plate is constructed of reflex reflecting material the letters and figures must be black, and the front number must have a white reflex reflecting background and the rear a yellow reflex reflecting background. It is submitted that these paragraphs [paragraphs 6, 7 and 8 of Part II of Schedule 2] do not prohibit a vehicle first registered prior to 1 January 1973 from displaying a white plate in front and a black one at the rear or a black plate in front and a yellow one at the rear, otherwise there would be the absurd result that, while a vehicle with black plates front and rear would be legal, one with a white plate in front and a black at the rear (or a black in front and a yellow at the rear) would not, notwithstanding that the white and yellow plates are easier to see than the black and consequently the vehicle would be safer than one with two black plates.'

If you can understand what that means, you are a better man than I am, Gunga Din.

Nowadays, personalized number plates have become very popular with egotistic drivers and you can easily buy yours from the DVLA. It even puts out a helpful free booklet, *Registration Numbers and You*, obtainable on request (see **Useful Addresses**). But back in December 1973 a woman called Jayne Lawn went about things the wrong way and was convicted of displaying illegally positioned marks contrary to the 1971 Regulations. She had moved a bolt half an inch so that it read L1 1AWN instead of the correct L11 AWN.

More recently, in February 1999, the DVLA announced a police campaign targeted at motorists who changed the spacing or shape of characters on their number plates – not just to read like their own name but to make up so-called 'funny' words. Examples were CAR 117S which became CARATS and RUB 818H which became RUBBISH. Such antics were not only childish but made cars difficult to trace and unidentifiable on speed cameras. Offenders were warned that they faced fines of up to £1,000 for breach of the 1971 Regulations – and quite right too.

It is also an offence not to keep your plates clean or undamaged so as to be clearly legible at all times.

O

ODD CASES

There is no shortage of them! Just consider the following few examples.

A delivery driver in Sheffield was given a £40 fixed penalty by police because his car's tinted windscreen was too dark. He had found the windows of his Ford Sierra were fitted with a stick-on film when he bought it. 'The car has a good stereo and I thought the windows would stop people seeing it,' he told the police. But his darkened windscreen let in only 20 per cent of light – and the legal minimum is 25 per cent.

A dairy farmer near Huddersfield found himself in his local magistrates' court after his cows did what cows do naturally as they crossed a road. A former police officer riding a motorcycle skidded on a cow pat and crashed, starting a legal battle which cost taxpayers more than £3,000. The farmer was charged with depositing slurry on a highway contrary to Section 161 of the 1980 Highway Act – but the magistrates cleared him after they agreed that it was his cows and not he who had deposited the offending matter.

A woman driver in Surrey was prosecuted at Wallington Magistrates' Court because the 'L' plates on the driving-school car in which she was taking her lessons were too large. In fact, they were nearly three times the regulation size. 'They gave an exemplary warning to the world,' her solicitor told the Bench, and they gave her a conditional discharge. But her driving instructor was fined £1 for aiding and abetting her.

Two police officers in Mid Glamorgan saw a man hanging drunkenly from the side of his four-wheel electric wheelchair as he drove the 2 miles home from a public house. He was an ex-painter crippled with arthritis and, when stopped, he refused to take a breath test. Bridgend magistrates gave him a twelve-month driving ban and fined him £200 but a more generous-hearted Crown Court judge later overturned the sentence. He ruled that the policemen did not have sufficient reason to believe that the man had been drink-driving.

A thirty-two-year-old financial adviser found by police slumped over the steering-wheel of a friend's stationary Mercedes at 4.40 a.m. had an unusual defence when charged at Dundee Sheriff Court with drink-driving, taking the car without its owner's consent and driving without insurance. He claimed that he had been sleepwalking! Sheriff Alan Finlayson accepted that was true – and that he had driven a mile from his home while apparently asleep. But he still convicted him and banned him from driving for a year because his automotive state was 'self-induced': he knew – or should have remembered – that previous sleepwalking incidents had been triggered by taking large quantities of alcohol.

OVERSEAS DRIVING

Many motorists enjoy taking their car to the Continent for a touring holiday. Personally, I adore it. But what about the local motoring laws? Even within the fifteen states of the European Union, laws vary considerably. Sometimes it is not enough just to be a good driver. You need to know instinctively how to react to local conditions. It helps to know the country's legal framework, too. These thoughts were sparked by the introduction of tough new speeding laws in France in the summer of 1998.

The death rate on the French roads is double that in Britain, even though the two countries have roughly the same populations. According to the French Transport Ministry, speed is largely to blame. So they brought in a new law. A fine of up to FF10,000 (about £1,000) was introduced for excessive speeding, defined as more than 48 kph (30 mph) over the limit.

Nowadays, holidaymakers pulled over for speeding by the French police can expect an on-the-spot fine of FF600 (£60) if they exceed the limit by 'only' up to 40 kph (25 mph). But if driving more than 48 kph (30 mph) over the limit, they also face this extra fine plus a court case.

How do you know what the limit is on a particular stretch of road in France? Here is the general rule: in a built-up area, it is 50 kph (31 mph); outside a built-up area, it is 90 kph (55 mph); on a dual carriageway, 110 kph (68 mph); and on a motorway, 130 kph (80 mph).

If you are pulled over, you cannot use the excuse that

lots of French drivers around you were travelling far faster than that! Not many Britons drive fast on the Continent anyway, but in France and Germany you should still keep your eyes open for local speed-limit variations. These are not usually signposted separately – you will find them on the place-name signs as you enter villages and small towns.

But enough of this doom and gloom. Driving on the Continent can be fun. Just remember that the drink-driving limit is often lower than in Britain. If in any doubt as to any country's motoring laws, it is always worthwhile checking before departure with its London embassy or a motoring organization of which you are a member. Here are some basic rules to bear in mind.

GB sticker

The AA maintains that on the Continent fines are still imposed for failing to display a nationality plate. Personally, I'm not so sure and, after much research, I still cannot point to any national or EU law which specifies that you must carry one. It has been claimed that this derives from the UN Convention on International Road Traffic, dating back to September 1949 – but I am by no means convinced.

Headlights

It is usually an offence not to adjust these for driving on the right-hand side of the road. You can buy beam converters from the AA or RAC at ports and at the entrance to the Channel Tunnel.

Driving licence and vehicle registration document ('log book')

Always have these in your car when driving, together with your passport and, if you have one, an international driving permit: the latter is useful, though not a legal necessity. Italy and Austria require, as well as a full driving licence, an official translation and an international permit. In France and Portugal, a driver whose full licence is less than two years or one year old respectively must observe lower speed limits. These are often not signposted, so newly qualified motorists should check before departure with either the appropriate London embassy or the AA or RAC.

Insurance

Third-party cover is a minimum legal requirement throughout the European Union. Always take your insurance certificate with you – after checking that your insurance still applies when driving abroad.

Green Card

Technically, you do not need this but I always ask my insurance broker for one – and sign it immediately. French entry police sometimes demand to see one and it can smooth your passage with local police in the event of an accident.

Bail Bond

I used always to take one out before driving in Spain. Although it was not a legal necessity, it was supposed to save you from being thrown into prison if you killed or injured someone accidentally. Views differ as to whether it is still required but, to be on the safe side, I usually still get one.

First aid kit and warning triangle

In many countries, you must carry these in case of an emergency.

Children

Children are not allowed to travel as front-seat passengers in most countries unless an approved child safety seat or restraint adapted to their size is fitted.

On-the-spot fines

In most European countries, the police can impose and collect these for speeding and minor offences. It is generally useless to argue – but always insist on getting a receipt.

Finally, as I once discovered on a remote mountain road in southern Spain: if you are stopped on the Continent, you are not allowed time to produce your driving licence, insurance certificate or vehicle registration document at a police station later. So keep these with you wherever you go – and never leave them in an unattended vehicle.

OVERTAKING

Is overtaking on your nearside illegal or merely bad driving practice? Surprisingly, there is no absolute rule against
it, even in the Highway Code. So what exactly is the law?

There is no straightforward answer. Let us start with the
Highway Code. Unfortunately, it is vague in the extreme.

For ordinary roads, it says: 'Only overtake on the left if
the vehicle in front is signalling to turn right, and there is
room to do so; . . . stay in your lane if traffic is moving
slowly in queues. If the queue on your right is moving
more slowly than you are, you may pass on the left .' And
for motorways: 'Overtake only on the right . . . Do not
move to a lane on your left to overtake.' And much more
in a similar vein.

Yet this partial acceptance of the practice is legally only
'advice'. It does not have the force of law. Section 38 of the
1988 Road Traffic Act states clearly: 'A failure on the part of
a person to observe a provision of the Highway Code shall
not of itself render that person liable to criminal proceedings
but any such failure may in any proceedings (whether civil
or criminal) be relied upon as tending to establish or nega-
tive any liability in question in those proceedings.' In other
words, if, for example, you have an accident on a motorway
when overtaking on the nearside and there is no slower-
moving queue of traffic on your right, that could help to
prove you were guilty of careless driving and liable to be
fined in a criminal court, or driving negligently and liable
to be ordered to pay damages in a civil court.

Overtaking

...at the Code says only has the force of law when it ...ely repeats what is already law because of some ...cific Act or Government regulation. It then uses the formula 'YOU MUST' or 'YOU MUST NOT'. The only occasions when it uses either version with regard to over-taking is on ordinary roads: 'You MUST NOT overtake if you would have to cross or straddle double white lines with a solid line nearest to you; if you would have to enter an area designed to divide traffic, if it is surrounded by a solid white line; the nearest vehicle to a pedestrian crossing, especially when it has stopped to let pedestrians cross; if you would have to enter a lane reserved for buses, trams or cycles during its hours of operation; after a "No Overtaking" sign and until you pass a sign cancelling the restriction.'

And with motorways it merely says: 'You MUST NOT use the hard shoulder for overtaking.' Big deal! Everyone knows that you can only use the hard shoulder for any purpose in an emergency anyway.

On many stretches of Britain's overcrowded motorways, traffic is constantly moving in queues. So a growing num-ber of drivers think this justifies their overtaking in the 'slower' lane – even though the car in front might choose that very moment to move into that lane. In 1998, a DETR spokesman suggested allowing overtaking in any lane on a motorway – as in the United States – but after the usual round of consultations with interested parties, the idea was dropped. In the words of an AA spokesman, overtaking on the left is 'extremely dangerous and puts other road users at risk'. Many motorists will surely agree. Personally

I have always thought of it as the hallmark of a particularly big-headed and selfish kind of driver.

Yet he breaks no law. So long as he does so safely – or you get out of the way in time – he can drive badly with legal impunity, despite the fact that the full definition of the offence of careless driving in Section 3 of the 1988 Road Traffic Act is 'driving without due care and attention *or without reasonable consideration for other persons using the road* [my italics]'.

Furthermore, many motorists think – or like to think – that 'audacious' overtaking, to use no stronger word, can only get you into trouble with the law if it causes an accident. No way. As far back as 1974, the High Court ruled in *Trentham* v. *Rowlands* that a motorway driver overtaking on the nearside can be guilty of dangerous driving because of the potential danger, even though no accident was caused.

Examples where overtaking can be an offence in itself are as follows.

- If you would have to cross or straddle double white lines with a solid line nearest to you *except* when safe to do so and you need to enter adjoining premises or a side road or pass a stationary vehicle or pedal cycle, horse or road maintenance vehicle travelling at 10 mph or less, to avoid an accident or comply with a direction by a uniformed police constable or traffic warden.

- You are overtaking another approaching vehicle within

the limits of a pedestrian crossing or stopped to let
pedestrians cross.

- After a 'No Overtaking' sign until passing another sign
  cancelling the restriction.

- If it means you have to drive on a motorway hard
  shoulder.

Finally, of course, we all remember from our learning-
to-drive days the famous old Highway Code rules, such as
not to overtake when approaching a corner or bend, a
hump bridge or the brow of a hill.

The basic rule, though slightly reworded in the latest
(1998) Highway Code, is: 'Overtake only when it is safe to
do so.' The Code also now emphasizes the danger of
overtaking on the left: 'Only overtake on the left,' states
Rule 139, 'if the vehicle in front is signalling to turn right,
and there is room to do so. Stay in your lane if traffic
is moving slowly in queues. If the queue on your right is
moving more slowly than you are, you may pass on the
left.'

People sometimes forget that two drivers are involved
in the act of overtaking: the overtaker and the overtaken.
Rule 104 in the previous (1996) Highway Code only
amounted to two short sentences. Rule 144 in the 1998
edition is much more specific: 'If a driver is trying to
overtake you, maintain a steady course and speed, slowing
down if necessary to let the vehicle pass. Never obstruct
drivers who wish to pass. Speeding up or driving unpre-

dictably while someone is overtaking you is dangerous.
Drop back to maintain a two-second gap if someone over-
takes and pulls into the gap in front of you.'

But the little-known 1994 Appeal Court case of *Smith* v.
Cribben would seem to throw this exemplary principle into
some doubt.

A stretch of dual carriageway, part of the Snodland
bypass in Kent, was narrowing to a single-file, two-lane
road ahead. Yet a woman motorist in the offside lane of
the soon-to-end dual carriageway chose that moment to
try to overtake a man in the nearside lane. What did
the nearside driver do? He did not slow down to let the
overtaking vehicle pass, and pull in. He did not even, as
many other motorists might have done, quickly accelerate
so that the would-be overtaker would have to pull back
because she was running out of space.

Instead, he kept going at the same speed. Unfortunately,
the overtaker did not pull back. She collided with oncoming traffic and was badly hurt. She then sued the nearside
driver for damages in the High Court, saying it was all his
fault. She claimed he had deliberately prevented her from
overtaking. Mr Justice Otton ruled that was not so but
stated that merely keeping a steady speed and not deceler-
ating was sufficiently negligent to make him 25 per cent
responsible for the accident.

The Appeal Court disagreed on the basis that the
woman driver had created the potential danger by persistently attempting to overtake when the dual carriageway
was ending – and that the motorist in the nearside lane
was not guilty of any negligence. Lord Justice Roch laid

down this – to my mind – questionable doctrine: 'The
ordinary reasonable driver cannot be expected to anticipate
that the following driver will drive dangerously and to
extricate that driver from the dangerous situation which
that driver creates. The onus on him is to drive normally
at a proper speed, on a proper course.'

With respect, the logic is not very persuasive. Is there
not also a duty on the part of the 'ordinary reasonable
driver' to do all he reasonably can to avoid accidents? If
another motorist is driving badly, surely you should react
and not simply continue as if nothing untoward was
happening?

P

PARKING

Since July 1994, most illegal parking in London has been 'decriminalized' and is no longer dealt with by police officers or traffic wardens. Save for parking dangerously, on zigzag lines or on red routes, or causing an obstruction, law enforcement has been handed over to uniformed parking attendants employed by the thirty-three London borough councils. A similar system may eventually spread throughout England and Wales but so far only Winchester, Oxford, High Wycombe and Maidstone have followed suit.

Under this scheme, the normal fixed penalty system does not apply. You either pay direct to the local council a penalty charge (no longer called a fine) which, on average, is £80 for central London and £60 for outer London and elsewhere, with a 50 per cent discount for paying within fourteen days. If the full amount is still unpaid within a *further* fourteen days, the council claims for it, as a civil debt, in a County Court.

If you believe that a parking attendant has wrongly or even unfairly given you a parking ticket (now called a penalty charge notice), you can write to the local council arguing that it should be withdrawn (see **Court Cases**). From personal experience, I know that this sometimes succeeds. But if the council rejects your plea, it must send you a form explaining you can appeal to a panel of independent adjudicators. This is a free and informal service available either in person or through the post.

Schedule 6 of the 1991 Road Traffic Act specifies the possible grounds of appeal: you were not the owner of the vehicle; you had ceased to be the owner before the alleged contravention or became the owner after that date; the vehicle had been parked by someone without your consent; the local 'No Waiting' order was invalid; you are a hire firm and the driver had accepted responsibility for any penalty charge; the penalty charge exceeded the permitted amount; and the alleged contravention 'did not occur'. This last ground of appeal can sometimes be generously interpreted and successful cases include those of a pregnant mother who could not walk far and had vainly searched for a legitimate parking place, and of an elderly man with a prostate problem who had to park illegally to visit a public convenience urgently. And there was one marvellous case in the London borough of Lambeth where a motorist checked with his tape measure after being booked by a parking attendant because one tyre of his Saab 900 overlapped by a mere inch or so a parking bay's outer white line. He found that the bay was too small to comply with the council's own 'No Waiting' regulations! So an independent adjudicator quashed the £30 penalty charge and awarded him £500 costs.

As so often in the law, you must be prepared to make an effort to gain justice. It does not always come easily.

With parking meters and pay-and-display areas, you

must buy on arrival all the time you want (usually up to two hours), with no time allowed for finding change and, of course, you cannot later 'feed the meter' or buy a second display voucher. Nor can you park on a meter showing 'Out of order' or covered by an official 'No Parking' bag. As for using unexpired time on a meter, the legal position is rather bizarre: you cannot 'feed the meter' so as to increase your allotted time (you will have to drive around and come back to the meter hoping that no one else has taken the space!) but someone else can legally use your unexpired time and reduce accordingly the amount of money that he puts into the meter! (See **Meters**).

Illegal parking can also lead to towing away and – so far only in London – to clamping (see **Towing Away and Clamping**).

PART-EXCHANGE

A reader in Winchester wrote to me once with a specific question after a 'Street Legal' on buying a used car: 'Can you still make the dealer take back an unsatisfactory vehicle if he has taken another vehicle or vehicles in part-exchange?'

I was happy to reply that the answer was 'Yes'. One's right under the 1979 Sale of Goods Act, as amended in 1994, to return a car not of 'satisfactory quality' if things go wrong within a reasonably short time (apart from obvious defects or those pointed out before purchase) is unaffected by part-exchange. That is merely a matter of how you agreed to pay for the vehicle. It does not alter the fact that there has been a 'sale of goods' with all its usual legal consequences. A sale is a sale.

PEDESTRIANS

If a pedestrian suddenly appears in front of you from between parked vehicles, what is your legal liability if you run into him?

This is a perennial problem and a judge's first question would be: 'What was your speed?' Paragraph 104 of the Highway Code makes clear: 'The speed limit is the absolute maximum and does not mean it is safe to drive at that speed irrespective of conditions.' A motorist is not expected never to have accidents but the law requires him not to have accidents that reasonable care would have avoided. That is why the expression often used by judges when exonerating a driver is: 'He did everything that a prudent motorist could have done to try to avoid the accident.'

Judge Stockdale said exactly that at Watford County Court in a 1996 case where a man delivering newspapers to a newsagent from a parked van on the other side of the road had suddenly appeared from behind a stationary bus. The bus driver had flashed his lights at him – which he took as an invitation to step into the road. But a motorcyclist was overtaking the bus. He was doing no more than 15 mph and he braked and swerved – but still hit the pedestrian. The motorcyclist's reasonable speed on a busy road plus his immediate – albeit unsuccessful – evasive action resulted in the injured delivery man losing his claim for damages.

But does it make any difference if the person suddenly appearing in traffic is a young child?

The law is ambivalent. On the one hand, it says that you cannot expect a child to be as careful as an adult. As Lord Denning said when a thirteen-year-old girl recovered damages after being hit by a car travelling 'at an excessive speed' on a busy London main road after she had stepped out from behind a stationary lorry, 'A very young child cannot be guilty of contributory negligence.'

So is there no legal protection for motorists at risk from young pedestrians injured through their own (understandable) foolhardiness?

The 'Green Cross Code' in the Highway Code says that children should be taught how to cross the road and that parents should not allow them out alone until it is safe to do so. But we all know that some modern parents fail their own children. In theory, the law remains the same for all pedestrians, adults and children: a motorist will only be liable if he has not done everything that a prudent driver would have done.

But there seems to be considerable judicial sympathy for motorists. For instance, a six-year-old boy visiting a sweet shop with his fourteen-year-old uncle suddenly ran into the road on his own from between parked cars and collided with a car on the other side of the road. His counsel argued that, seeing children in that busy shopping street, the driver should have been travelling more slowly and keeping a better look-out so that he could have braked well before the little boy had reached the centre of the road. He should also have sounded his horn. The judge dismissed his claim, and the Appeal Court upheld the judge.

The appeal judges ruled that there was nothing to show that the motorist had been driving at an improper speed, and the fact that he was unable to stop in time, even though on the other side of the road, was not, in itself, a reason for saying that in every case of that sort, a motorist should have been able to avoid an accident.

PENALTY POINTS

When an offence is sufficiently major to warrant a licence being endorsed (see **Vital Legal Terms**), the court may also impose 'penalty points'. These are valid for three years, although after four years (eleven years with drink-driving) you can send your licence to the DVLA at Swansea and ask them to re-issue it with the points deleted – which is always worth doing. It can be psychologically useful to show a police officer, if stopped, a beautifully clean licence.

As we will see in **Totting Up**, acquiring too many penalty points can lead to disqualification if you commit an offence which 'tots up' to twelve the points incurred over the past three years up to your latest offence.

How many points are likely in any particular case? It varies. Less serious offences (defective tyres, failing to comply with traffic lights, etc.) carry their own fixed number of points, usually three. But more serious offences have a range where a court can select how many it considers appropriate to the facts of that particular case. The complete list of penalty points is as follows.

OFFENCE	PENALTY POINTS
Being in charge of a motor vehicle when unfit through drink/drugs	10
Failing to provide a specimen of breath for analysis	3–11
Failing to provide a roadside breath test	4
Being in charge of a motor vehicle with excess alcohol in breath/blood/urine	10
Driving when unfit through drink/drugs	10
Driving with excess alcohol in breath/blood/urine	3–11
Aggravated vehicle-taking	3–11
Careless driving	3–9
Causing death by careless driving when under the influence of drink or drugs	3–11
Causing death by dangerous driving	3–11
Construction and use offences where a motor vehicle's condition, load, use, etc., cause danger of injury	3
Dangerous driving	3–11
Driving after losing licence on medical grounds	3–6

OFFENCE	PENALTY POINTS
Driving otherwise than in accordance with driving licence	3–6
Driving while disqualified	6
Failing to comply with traffic lights	3
Failing to comply with traffic/police signs	3
Failing to identify driver of a vehicle	3
Failing to report an accident when required to do so	5–10
Failing to stop after an accident	5–10
No insurance	6–8
Parking in a dangerous position	3
Parking within the confines of a pedestrian crossing	3
Speeding	3*
Speeding if convicted in court	3–6
Defective brakes	3*
Defective steering	3*
Defective tyres*	3

* fixed penalty

NOTE: When several offences are committed at the same time, only the largest number of points awarded for one of those offences will count. For example, passing a red light and speeding while having defective tyres are three separate offences and could earn a total of up to twelve points. But only the most points given for any one of them – perhaps six for speeding – will be taken into account.

PETROL

On 1 January 2000, the EU banned the sale of leaded petrol
for health and environmental reasons. Of the 21 million
cars in the United Kingdom, 7.25 million had been using
leaded petrol. So what could they legally turn to?
Unleaded petrol was the obvious alternative but something
called 'LAP' began to appear on service station forecourts.
It stood for lead replacement petrol and met with a varied
response from motorists. The AA even set up a help-line
on 0990 500600 to advise its members on adjustments
which they might need to make to their car engines after
so many years of only using leaded petrol. However, the
only people now allowed to buy leaded petrol are owners
of classic racing cars – but they cannot buy it from forecourts.

PETROL PUMPS

Are petrol stations under a legal duty to signpost ade-
quately their various pumps?

I always thought that, on general principles, the answer
must be 'Yes' but, until a 1996 small claims court case, I
could not go further. Forty-two-year-old schoolteacher
Chris Davenport had pulled into his local Ads service
station at Leamington Spa to fill up his Renault 18 in order
to drive to Birmingham for a job interview and, in his own

words, 'grabbed what I thought was the petrol pump, shoved it in, filled up, paid and drove off'. Within 300 yards, the car began to cough and splutter. He limped home and called the RAC. When he told the patrolman what had happened, the man's face broke into a broad smile. He realized at once what had happened. He disconnected the fuel pipe and found that Mr Davenport had filled his car's tank with diesel. 'Admittedly, I was in a tearing hurry,' Mr Davenport explained, 'but there was only a little notice, which I did not see, saying the pump contained diesel.'

It cost him £55 to get the tank put right – and he did not get the job. So he complained to Ads, which referred him to its insurers. He also contacted consumer advisers who, he said, told him that about ten other motorists had made a similar error at the same supermarket. He took his case to a small claims court and Ads offered £400 in settlement, which he accepted.

An Ads spokesman defended the pump design. 'They are very clearly marked, on the nozzle and at the side of the pump,' he said. But the fact remains that his company chose to pay out to this dissatisfied customer and, although no legally binding precedent was laid down because there was no formal adjudication by a district judge (and, in any event, small claims courts count as private arbitrations and not as full court proceedings), a valuable pointer was set for the future. Petrol stations are under a legal duty to take reasonable care in the design and layout of their forecourt pumps so that motorists are not misled into putting into their tanks the wrong grade of petrol, or diesel instead of petrol (or vice versa).

PHONES

When the latest (1998) edition of the Highway Code appeared in the shops in February 1999 after the previous update six years earlier, for the first time it gave a stern warning to motorists who combined driving with talking on the phone. It said specifically that drivers should never make or receive calls on a hand-held phone and also strongly advised against use of a hands-free instrument.

In fact, although there is no such offence as using a phone while driving, it can easily form the basis of at least three other offences, depending on the seriousness of the circumstances: careless driving, dangerous driving and even causing death through dangerous driving. But it is wrong to say, as is sometimes claimed in the Press, that the police cannot charge drivers simply for using a mobile phone and that they must prove either careless or dangerous driving. That is nonsense. They can, and do, prosecute drivers under Regulation 104 of the 1986 Road Vehicles (Construction and Use) Regulations for not being in proper control of their motor vehicle (see **Careless Driving** and **Proper Control**).

It is, after all, basic common sense as well as good driving practice to remain in proper control of your vehicle at all times, and not do anything to take your mind off the road – such as nattering on the phone.

PHOTOGRAPHS

They can sometimes help you win your case, as Labour MP Ann Clwyd found in 1997 when she produced in court photographs successfully challenging whether police officers in their patrol car could really have seen what they claimed to have seen when booking her for 'jumping the lights'.

Miss Clwyd won her case and the Cardiff stipendiary magistrate, Richard Cox, said, 'I find myself in a position where there is an element of doubt, and I must give the benefit of that doubt to the defendant.' This was a highly articulate woman, unfazed by the court surroundings, fighting her own corner – and backed up by her photographs.

If it had been word against word, I am not at all sure – with great respect to Miss Clwyd – that the result would have been the same. It is simply not good enough to say, 'I shall tell the truth on oath. They must believe me.' It does not always work out like that. In my earlier days at the Bar when I used to do a lot of motoring work, I always advised clients, where necessary, to go back to the scene of the alleged offence and take photographs. It helped me to win quite a few cases.

POLICE CARS AND OTHER EMERGENCY SERVICE VEHICLES

In my 'Street Legal' in June 1999 I wrote about the increasing concern that innocent motorists and other road users were being killed or injured by police drivers on duty.

Statistics showed that in the twelve months from 1 April 1998 to 31 March 1999, twenty-two people had been killed in accidents involving police vehicles, with four people killed in the first eight weeks of 1999 alone. Of the twenty-two who had died, seventeen were killed in high-speed pursuits of suspected criminals whilst the five others were killed by cars answering emergency calls.

Since 1993 no fewer than 120 people have been killed and 11,000 injured by speeding police cars. That was a staggering statistic. So I asked the question: are police drivers – and ambulance and fire engine drivers – above the law?

The answer is both 'Yes' and 'No'. In general, drivers in these special categories enjoy no specific privileges. When it comes to civil liability to pay compensation to anyone injured by their negligent driving, their legal position is the same as any other motorist's. Back in May 1959, in the leading case of *Gaynor* v. *Allen*, Mr Justice McNair laid down in the High Court the basic rule for all drivers of emergency service vehicles, although his decision in terms applied only to the police. A police motorcyclist had been chasing a speeding motorist at some 60 mph along the

Great West Road at Hammersmith, London, where the legal limit was only 40 mph, when he crashed into a woman crossing the road. Awarding her damages for her injuries, Mr Justice McNair said, 'This police driver must, as regards civil liability, be judged in exactly the same way as any other driver. Like any other driver of a motor vehicle, he owed a duty to the public to drive with due care and attention and without exposing the members of the public to unnecessary danger.'

But when it comes to the question of whether or not a motoring offence has been committed, criminal law creates three specific exemptions when a vehicle is 'being used for fire brigade, ambulance or police purposes'.

Section 87 of the 1984 Road Traffic Regulation Act states that the speed limit does not apply to such a vehicle. As in *Gaynor* v. *Allen*, a speeding driver may have to pay damages, if a judge later rules that his speeding amounted to negligent driving in all the circumstances – which will usually include whether his sirens were blaring or his blue light was flashing. But, whatever the circumstances, he cannot be charged with the criminal offence of exceeding the speed limit.

Regulation 15 of the 1994 Traffic Signs Regulations and General Directions states that the driver of a police car or other emergency service vehicle may ignore 'Keep Left' and 'Keep Right' signs – but only in a manner or at a time likely not to endanger anyone.

Regulation 33 states the same for traffic lights at red. This means that a police driver cannot be prosecuted for failing to obey the traffic lights – but he can be prosecuted for dangerous or careless driving if, for instance, he causes an accident.

There is no legal *carte blanche* for drivers of emergency service vehicles to disregard red traffic lights or any other road sign. As *Roadcraft*, the police drivers' official handbook, states in its latest (1997) edition: 'Your overriding responsibility in any situation is to drive safely, and that is what you should be thinking about while you are driving to an emergency. If you have an accident and you fail to arrive, you are no help to the people in need.'

That is, of course, an admirable concept. But, in practice, speeding police drivers can often expect to receive sympathetic consideration by prosecutors and judges.

The pattern was set in May 1994 in the case of a police marksman called out – on what later turned out to be a hoax – to intercept armed robbers. He sped through a red traffic light on the A4 at Benham Hill, Thatcham, Berks, and collided with another car. Its twenty-seven-year-old driver was killed. At Reading Crown Court, the marksman was acquitted of causing death by dangerous driving after Mr Justice Popplewell ruled that the prosecution had not proved he had been driving at 'far below the standards of a normal driver'. He was fined £100 after admitting a lesser charge of careless driving. The judge told him: 'This was an emergency which required a speedy response. You were exhibiting warning lights and the siren was going, and you were clearly seen and heard by a number of witnesses.'

Perhaps understandably the dead man's father said that he was disgusted with the judge's decision which, he claimed, gave police officers the right to 'kill at random'.

Mercifully, that so-called right is unknown to the law and occasionally police drivers who kill innocent people find themselves jailed. This happened in February 1997 to a police driver who killed two people after 'shooting' a red light while chasing after a stolen Ford Escort driven by a sixteen-year-old. Jailing him for three months at Birmingham Crown Court for causing death through dangerous driving, the Recorder, Peter Crawford, said he did not relish the task but 'this is a matter this court cannot overlook'.

If any charge at all is brought, however, the Crown Prosecution Service is more likely to sandpaper it down to careless driving. Faced with an upsurge in accidents, some police forces are now said to be contemplating various measures designed to ensure the better management of high-speed police chases; and one must always have sympathy for police officers acting in pursuance of their duty.

NOTE: In October 2000, the Metropolitan Police announced that 3,000 police cars in the London police area were to be fitted with airplane-style 'black boxes' to monitor drivers' and other crew members' performance in the last moments before a crash.

PRIVATE CLAMPING

Despite official promises, the Denver cowboys still have a licence to bill. What is the latest state of play on wheel-clamping on private land?

In England and Wales there is still no Government

reform of the law which, as the RAC has said more than once, means there is plenty of money to be made by the clamper but little protection for the motorist who gets clamped. This is not the case in Scotland where (and I write as a non-Scotsman) the law is often so much more sensible. In June 1992, the Court of Session in Edinburgh declared wheel clamping on private land illegal as 'extortion and theft'.

Yet south of the Border, despite a so-called commitment from the Home Office to look into pirate clamping 'with all urgency' in 1992, full official consultations in 1993 and a valiant attempt by backbench MPs to insert a regulatory clause into the Criminal Justice Bill in 1994, years later 'urgent' – or, indeed, any – action still remains to be taken.

Any unscrupulous person with a mobile phone, intimidating staff and a set of clamps, employed by a private landowner, can earn himself up to £250 a time in browbeating innocent motorists.

Just look at the following typical cases.

Clampers in Doncaster threaten to hold a mother's three-year-old daughter ransom until she collects £60 from the bank. Clampers in Sheffield demand a female motorist's gold tooth as payment for parking on waste land. Clampers in North Yorkshire force two pensioners to hand over their pensions before releasing their cars. Clampers in Slough force a pregnant woman to walk 3 miles to obtain cash before releasing her car.

As the motoring organizations and the Consumers' Association all agree, the remedy would be simple: private landowners would be allowed to permit clamping only if they obtained from their local authority a licence which obliged them to employ contractors operating to a strict code of conduct.

All other clamping on private land would be illegal, as in Scotland. Fine. But no one can give any actual date as to when such a system is likely to come into force. Meanwhile, what can the motorist do to protect himself?

Here are my suggestions. Before parking on private land (which includes apparently waste land), look carefully to see if there are any warning signs – however small or partly covered by foliage. If you see one, on no account park there. If you do, you will be asking for trouble. If you are clamped, insist that the clamper shows you his written authority from the landowner to clamp on that particular piece of land. Without such authority, he is acting illegally, even in the present unsatisfactory state of English law. So, if he cannot produce this authority, call the police and report him for the offence of trying to obtain money by deception. Not many motorists realize that as far back as May 1993, two men, operating as a 'security company', were found guilty by High Wycombe magistrates of obtaining money by deception after demanding payment for releasing twenty-three cars clamped without the landowner's permission on local waste land. They were fined a total of £3,640 and ordered to pay £1,399 compensation plus £75 costs.

If you find yourself clamped, note the name and address of the clamping company, its employee and the landowner and obtain a receipt for any money paid. But do not attempt, in your anger, to remove the clamp yourself.

Legally it belongs to the clamper and you could find that he reports you to the police for the offence of criminal damage.

If you consider that you have been unfairly clamped or have paid an excessive release fee, consult your motoring organization or a solicitor. They may advise you to sue in your local small claims court. Often clampers do not bother to defend and you get your money back – plus your court fee – by default without even having to go to court.

Back in November 1995, the Appeal Court made a ruling in *Arthur* v. *Anker* that was supposed to clarify and even, to some extent, strengthen drivers' rights. But, in practice, it has proved of limited effect.

The appeal judges refused to follow the Scottish Court of Session's earlier ruling that wheel-clamping on private land was illegal as 'extortion and theft'. Upholding a £40 charge for unclamping a Rover car in a private car park at Truro, the English judges held that a motorist who parks his car without permission on private land, despite having seen prominently displayed warning notices, voluntarily accepts the risk that his car may be clamped and remain immobilized until he pays a 'reasonable' fee.

Sir Thomas (now Lord) Bingham, then Master of the Rolls, explained that the Scottish court's decision did not apply in England because a clamper does not intend to deprive a motorist of his car permanently but only until his charges are paid, and so cannot be guilty, in English law, of theft. In Scotland, theft can be proved without any intention to deprive an owner permanently of his goods.

But he added: 'I would not accept that the clamper

could exact any unreasonable or exorbitant charge for releasing the car ... Nor may he justify detention of the car after the owner has indicated willingness to comply with the condition for release. He cannot justify any delay in releasing the car after the owner offers to pay and there must be means for the owner to communicate his offer.'

Those words could be of great value. They do not, in precise terms, say that a clamper must accept a cheque or, in the absence of cash, an offer to pay later supported by proper identification. But that seems to be implicit in the insistence on reasonableness. It therefore makes unlawful the earlier sharp practices we have already described, such as clampers demanding a female motorist's gold tooth in payment, or forcing a pregnant woman to walk 3 miles to obtain cash.

In that light, the ruling seems slowly to be having some effect. For instance, in Poole, Dorset, clampers working for a firm employed by the local council clamped a meals-on-wheels van as it was delivering food to pensioners and demanded £60 in cash from its seventy-two-year-old WRVS driver before releasing it. She had only £10 in cash and, despite the old folk waiting for their food, the clampers refused her offer to pay by cheque. Luckily, an onlooker cashed her cheque for her and the council later agreed to return the money and investigate the incident.

But abuses still regularly occur. The motoring organizations still frequently receive complaints from members who have been made to fork out up to £200 to get their car released. Some have had their cheques refused or have been forced to pay by credit card, with surcharges, while others have even been 'escorted' to cashpoint machines for the release fee. In some cases, quoting Lord Bingham's words, they might well have been able successfully to sue these cowboys for damages in their local small claims court. But so long as the law remains unclear and insufficiently well known, few people will bother with the time-consuming process of going to law, even when, as with the small claims system, lawyers' fees are not usually involved.

But in any case, why should it be left to private justice to curb clampers' excesses? Why does Parliament not enact straightforward, easily enforceable laws for the registration of all wheel-clampers, with stringent rules regulating their behaviour? Nothing can excuse the Home Office's amazing failure – in successive Tory and Labour administrations – to honour its early promise to look into private clamping 'with all urgency'. As Edmund King, head of campaigns at the RAC, has said, 'Cowboy clampers are getting away with legalized mugging.'

PROPER CONTROL

In June 2000, the police were not flavour of the month with many motorists, and two incidents showed why.

First, there was the case of thirty-three-year-old Kevin Storey, fined £20 on the spot for eating a KitKat at the wheel when driving on the M3 in Hampshire with his wife and children to a christening – even though he had asked his wife to unwrap the 30p snack for him while he kept his eyes on the road. There was an outcry in the Press. 'Excessive police zeal', claimed the Association of British Drivers, and the Hampshire Assistant Chief Constable cancelled the fixed penalty ticket as 'inappropriate action by a well-meaning officer'.

However, that was swiftly followed by the case of twenty-seven-year-old Linda Smart, also handed a £20 on-the-spot ticket – for drinking from a bottle of mineral water although her car was stationary at traffic lights in Chippenham, Wiltshire. She was so angered by the incident that she exercised her right to challenge her ticket in court. In the event, two months later, she ended up in Chippenham Magistrates' Court where she was convicted, fined £40 (as against a potential maximum of £1,000) and incurred £50 costs. The woman Chairman of the Bench explained: 'The reason we have come to this decision is that you started drinking while stationary and drove off with the bottle still in your hand. This proves you would not have been able to control your vehicle.'

And, indeed, that is the offence involved in both these cases: namely, 'Driving a motor vehicle on a road in such a position that the driver cannot have proper control of the vehicle', contrary to Regulation 104 of the 1986 Road Vehicles (Construction and Use) Regulations.

As an AA spokesman has commented, 'In the end, it is the policeman's call. If he considers that your driving has been impaired, whether it be from fiddling with your radio, looking at a map or eating, then he will stop you.'

We have all been taught to concentrate on what we are doing and to drive with both hands on the steering-wheel

in a 'ten to two' position. The many motorists who choose
to drive with only one hand firmly on the wheel and the
other hand lightly touching it, with one arm leaning casu-
ally out of the open window, are positively inviting a
certain type of police officer to stop and, at the very least,
rebuke them.

My own two favourite Regulation 104 cases are first,
that of the duke's daughter fined £75 for being locked in 'a
passionate embrace with her passenger' as she sped along
the fast lane on the M6. And second, that of the judge who,
on his way to Newcastle-upon-Tyne Crown Court, was
pulled in and later given a written caution for steering
with one hand and shaving with the other. At least he had
the grace to admit, 'It was a very silly thing to do.'

What about mobile phones? Many motorists believe that
driving with only one hand on the wheel and the other
holding a mobile phone is, in itself, perfectly legal and only
becomes an offence if an accident were to occur through
both hands not being on the wheel.

But, as we have seen under **Phones**, there does not have
to be an accident. Successful prosecutions have been
brought without one. In fact, the Hampshire police force
that cancelled Kevin Storey's ticket had just completed a
campaign targeting motorists using mobile phones – and
one can readily understand why. As Rule 127 of the latest
edition of the Highway Code states, 'You MUST exercise
proper control of your vehicle at all times. Never use a
hand-held mobile phone or microphone when driving.
Using hands-free equipment is also likely to distract your
attention from the road. It is far safer not to use any

telephone while you are driving – find a safe place to stop first.'

A car is a lethal weapon and, especially with modern traffic and crowded roads, driving cannot safely be combined with any other activity. Drivers without *both* hands on the wheel could also be prosecuted for driving without due care and attention and even for dangerous driving. This actually happened a couple of years ago when a policeman driving along the M4 was overtaken at 70 mph by a man reading a book propped open on the steering-wheel. He gave chase and the twenty-five-year-old executive was banned for three months and fined £250 with £400 costs at Cardiff Crown Court after admitting dangerous driving.

The question in each case is whether the police officer's action is reasonable in all the circumstances or an arrogant exercise of power.

Q

QUEASY OR TIRED

Motorways can be tiring places, especially on long journeys: so what is the law about pulling on to the hard shoulder to give yourself a rest if you begin to feel queasy or tired? Paragraph 7 of the 1982 Motorways Traffic (England and Wales) Regulations states that you can stop on a hard shoulder 'by reason of any accident, illness or other emergency', but – of course – does not say what an 'emergency' is.

In March 1992, thirty-seven-year-old High Wycombe antiques dealer Chris Timms was returning from a business visit to France. He was driving his Ford Transit van back home from Dover along the M25, having just passed the junction with the A3, when, at around midnight, his eyes 'suddenly started bouncing', as he told me later.

He realized he was a potential danger to other drivers and to himself. He thought it was too far to go to the next junction, so he pulled on to the hard shoulder, stopped, turned off the engine – leaving the lights on – and closed his eyes. Next thing he knew, a policeman was asking him why he had stopped. The sequel, despite a vigorous defence by Mr Timms acting as his own lawyer, was a £60 fine at Woking Magistrates' Court for stopping his vehicle contrary to the 1982 Regulations. In other words, his sudden tiredness was not an 'emergency'.

But, like all too many motorists found guilty in our magistrates' courts, he was left with a strong sense of grievance. 'What else could I have done that night?' he asked me. 'If you stop you're convicted of one offence, and if you carry on driving and crash into someone, you are convicted of a different, even more serious offence.'

So, still defending himself, he appealed to Guildford Crown Court where, in October 1992, Judge Peter Slot overruled his conviction. Awarding him £30 costs, Judge Slot said, 'I see no reason to reject Mr Timms's evidence that he felt tired after he passed a junction. It follows that what he did was within the law.'

His case has a wider implication for motorists. An anonymous 'legal expert' was quoted in several national newspapers at the time as saying, 'Motorists must understand that the law has not changed. The judge simply made an exception to the rule.' That was – and is – totally misleading. Judge Slot did not make an exception to the rule: he was applying and enforcing it.

For, as far back as February 1972, Lord Widgery, then Lord Chief Justice, in the High Court case of *Higgins* v. *Bernard*, brought on an earlier but identical version of the 1982 Regulations, authoritatively defined what is an 'emergency' for motorway drivers suddenly feeling ill or tired.

Taking as his basis the dictionary definition of 'emergency' as 'a sudden or unexpected occurrence', Lord Widgery said, 'Too much stress must not be attached to the word "sudden".' The tiredness does not have to attack the motorist at the very second before he pulls on to the hard shoulder.

Lord Widgery continued: 'If he gets on to the carriageway at a time when, as far as he could see, it was safe and lawful for him to proceed to the next turn-off point, the next thing to show is that something supervened – not necessarily some sudden exigency of the moment, but something intervened which rendered it unsafe to proceed to the next turn-off point.' So the reason why Judge Slot quashed Mr Timms's conviction was that he only felt tired after he had passed the M25's junction with the A3 and he was 'stuck', as it were, on the motorway until the next junction which was some distance ahead.

R

RANDOM TESTING

This subject is so important that I make no apologies for
returning to it in some depth, although I have briefly dealt
with it already in **Breath Tests** (and see also **Moving
Traffic Offence**). It may come as something of a surprise
to know that you can be lawfully breathalysed at random.
The popular view persists that the police can stop a motorist for suspected drink-driving only if he has committed a
'moving traffic offence' or been involved in an accident.
That is not true – and has not been true ever since the
little-known decision of *Harris* v. *Croson* in the run-up to
Christmas 1972. In that case, a motorist was stopped for
allegedly not displaying an up-to-date road fund licence.
The policeman smelt alcohol on his breath and promptly
tested him – to find that he was over the limit.

The magistrates ruled that the driver had been random-
tested and threw out the charge. But the police appealed
and Lord Widgery, then Lord Chief Justice, sitting with
two High Court judges in the Divisional Court, ruled: 'The
mere fact that a check can be described as random is no
ground for dismissing a drink-driving charge.' He pointed
out that the police (under what is now Section 163 of the
1988 Road Traffic Act) can legally stop a motorist on a

road at any time without having any particular reason. If, once they have done so, they smell alcohol on his breath – that's it! They can breathalyse him!

Yet how is that legally possible? When the breathalyser was introduced by the 1967 Road Safety Act, the Bill's first draft contained a clause permitting random testing but it was deleted after protests from the motoring organizations and the public at large who saw it as an unwarranted intrusion into their privacy. And in February 1991, a cross-party attempt to give police the power to hold random roadside breath tests was defeated by 265 votes to 157.

That was wasted parliamentary hot air. The judges have brought in by the back door what MPs have, at least twice, rejected, and done so by a marvellous piece of legal casuistry. In the subsequent Divisional Court case of *Chief Constable of Gwent* v. *Dash* in June 1985, Lord Justice Lloyd and Mr Justice Macpherson ruled that, although the law prohibited random breath tests, it did not prohibit random *stopping of cars*.

It is surprising that this judgment, like that of Lord Widgery and his colleagues, was reported in neither of the two major Law Reports but only in the specialized Road Traffic Reports. The facts were absolutely typical. At 11.15 p.m. on 25 April 1983, a motorist drove out from a public house in Blackwood, Gwent, and was stopped by a woman police officer, even though she had no grounds for suspecting him of having committed any moving traffic offence. She smelt alcohol on his breath and asked him to take a breath test. He was well over the limit and the local magistrates took away his driving licence for twelve months.

It was restored on appeal to Gwent Crown Court but Mr Justice Macpherson, with whom Lord Justice Lloyd agreed, ruled that the Crown Court judge had been wrong: 'There is no restriction upon the stopping of motorists by a policeman in the execution of his duty and the subsequent requirement for a breath test should the policeman then and there genuinely suspect the ingestion of alcohol. It may be said by some to be bad luck that such a situation arises but it is not unlawful provided the officer is in uniform and acts without . . . caprice or some false pretence or proved "malpractice".' Mr Justice Macpherson went on: 'Some will, of course, say that checks of this kind are invasions of liberty, but driving with too much alcohol in the blood is also a gross invasion of the rights of others.'

So there we have it.

REGISTERING YOUR CAR

When you buy a new car, you will be handed a registration document (the 'log book') giving particulars of the vehicle. You must insert your name and address as what the law calls the vehicle's registered keeper and post it to the DVLA. Thereafter, when you eventually sell the car, you should not hand over the log book privately – do not part with the document until you have been paid in full and the DVLA informed. If you carelessly hand it over to a new owner without ensuring that the log book with details of the new 'registered owner' is sent to the DVLA, you may find yourself liable for someone else's traffic offences!

(See **Buying a New Car.**)

REPLACEMENT CAR

If your car is damaged in an accident, when can you claim the cost of hiring a temporary replacement? The general principle has always been simple enough: in any case where you suffer injury or loss through someone else's negligence, they must pay compensation for the reasonably foreseeable consequences of their negligence.

So if a negligent driver damages your car, it is a 'reasonably foreseeable consequence' that (a) even if it is off the road for only a short time being repaired, you will suffer inconvenience for which you are entitled to be compensated, and (b) if the repairs take a long time, you will have to hire a temporary replacement for the cost of which you are entitled to be reimbursed.

Surprisingly, there was no authoritative legal ruling on hiring costs until June 1992, when the Appeal Court gave judgment in *Mattocks* v. *Mann*. Until then, any lawyer advising his client was thrown back on general legal waffle about 'reasonableness': the hired car had to be 'reasonably' similar to the damaged vehicle and you could only expect the negligent motorist (or his insurance company) to pay the full cost of hiring a replacement if your car was off the

road for a 'reasonable' time. Yet what exactly did that tired
and much over-used word mean in this context? In *Mattocks* v. *Mann*, an expectant mother's two-door Peugeot 205
was badly damaged through another woman driver's negligence in an accident in St Albans. No one disputed that
she needed a replacement during the six weeks the repairs
were expected to take – although, in fact, they took nearer
twelve weeks.

But two separate issues arose for decision.

The expectant mother hired a four-door Ford Sierra to
replace her damaged Peugeot 205 – and it had always only
been thought 'reasonable' to hire a two-door car to replace
a two-door car. So the other woman's insurance company
refused to pay the full cost. But Lord Justice Beldam said
they were wrong. There was no such general rule and he
emphasized that all these cases turn on their own facts.
Since the expectant mother had succeeded in renting a
four-door Ford Sierra for less than the cost of another two-
door Peugeot 205, it was 'quite impossible to say it was
unreasonable'. Size alone was not the criterion.

The insurance company did not pay the repairer's bill
until five months after the work was completed and,
during all that time, the woman continued to hire a
replacement. Was she saddled with her own hire bill
during all that time on the basis that it was, after all, legally
her bill for work done to her car, and the fact that she
could not afford to pay it herself and then get it back from
the insurance company was not the insurers' fault?

Again, Lord Justice Beldam decided against the insurers.
In words which deserve to be better known (again, the case

is not reported in the ordinary Law Reports but only in the specialized Road Traffic Reports – page 13 of the 1993 volume), he said, 'In these days when everybody looks to one or other of the insurers of vehicles involved in an accident, it is clearly contemplated that where the cost of repairs is of the substantial kind involved in this case, the source of payment of that cost will be the insurers.

'Looking at the whole history of events, one cannot isolate the plaintiff's inability to meet the cost of those repairs and say that that all brought to an end the period for which it was reasonable that the insurers should be liable.'

Every motorist – and motor insurance company – should realize that, if motorists act promptly in getting a damaged car to the repairers and informing the other driver's insurers, they should not be penalized because of the insurers' own unreasonable delay. And this also applies to delays caused by the insurers not authorizing repair work promptly in the first place.

RESIDENTS' PARKING PERMITS

These permits are something of a cheat because, as anyone who has paid good money to their local council to purchase one will know, they do not guarantee you a parking space. I do not think there is a local authority in the country that has an available parking bay for every resident's permit issued. Furthermore, permission to park in any specific bay can always be temporarily rescinded at the council's discretion. It is possible to come back and find that your car, legally parked in a resident's bay before you go on holiday, is not there when you get back – and you have to pay to recover it from the local pound.

A question that I am often asked is: Can anyone legally park out of hours in a resident's bay? As a general rule, the answer is 'Yes' – but, just in case, you should always look around for any contrary indication on an official time plate displayed on a nearby lamp-post. I was once caught out through not checking.

RETAKING THE DRIVING TEST

No one does this voluntarily and we have already seen that, when disqualifying for dangerous driving and causing death through dangerous driving, a court will order the defendant to take an extended driving test at the end of the disqualification.

There are two other instances when a court can order a motorist to be disqualified until he retakes his ordinary driving test. One is long-standing and the other is comparatively recent:

Section 36 of the 1988 Road Traffic Offenders Act, re-enacting earlier legislation, gives courts the power, with all endorsable offences, to re-order a driving test – when necessary for 'the safety of road users'. Yet, as Mr Justice Talbot ruled back in 1975, 'This is not a punitive power but should be used in respect of people who are growing old or infirm or show some incompetence in the offence which requires looking into.'

Undoubtedly, this will often involve elderly people whose ability to drive safely has been brought into question (see **Elderly Drivers**) but it can include unsafe or arrogant drivers of any age.

The 1995 Road Traffic (New Drivers) Act states that drivers who notch up six penalty points within two years of passing their driving test will have to take it again. According to the DETR, new drivers are twice as likely to have an accident as other motorists. 'This should make roads safer for all,' said a junior transport minister shortly before the Act became law.

Motoring law does not only punish, it also protects.

ROAD RAGE

As a legal concept, 'road rage' does not exist. Loss of temper, however violent, by a motorist involved in a driving incident is not an offence in itself. It can, however, be an ingredient in several other offences which may vary from a minor breach of the peace or public order offence, such as a rude gesture or offensive remark while at the wheel (which will seldom get to court), to dangerous driving, serious assaults or even, mercifully in rare cases, murder.

Most people believe road rage is a strictly modern

phenomenon. The term has been current in Britain for only about the past five years, and it is said to have been first used in April 1988 in the United States when a Florida newspaper reported that in a local court case, 'a fit of road rage has landed a man in jail'. But, of course, drivers have been losing their tempers with each other ever since the first motor cars trundled onto the roads. Yet it is undoubtedly true that only comparatively recently have so many cases occurred.

At first, the courts were slow to respond. They tended only to impose a fine and penalty points or perhaps a short disqualification. But in the past few years motorists who had never before seen the inside of a prison have begun to find themselves tasting the experience.

And not only men. As London stipendiary magistrate Mrs Ros Keating said in a recent case, 'Any kind of assault when someone is enraged on the road must result in prison. It happens far too often these days.' That was when a forty-nine-year-old businesswoman – presumably not usually a thug – had attacked a thirty-year-old woman journalist after a minor traffic incident in the respectable London area of Chelsea. She pulled her victim's hair, smacked her head against her car bonnet, then bit her above her right eyebrow. She was jailed for thirty days.

In another case, when jailing a sixty-nine-year-old pensioner for eighteen months for pulling out a folding knife and stabbing a forty-five-year-old motorist in a row about the older man's driving, Judge John Swanson said at Leeds Crown Court, 'Violence arising from disputes between motorists in cars will normally result in a prison sentence. When the facts are accompanied by a weapon, the sentence must be substantial.' It made no difference that the victim had brought the attack upon himself by chasing the pensioner to a car park because he thought that he had cut him up.

In January 1997, in the first 'road rage' case to reach the Appeal Court, Lord Bingham, then Lord Chief Justice, gave a lead to all other judges by increasing from six months to two years the prison sentence on a twenty-seven-year-old Manchester motorist who had seriously injured another driver and his passenger in a totally unjustified attack. 'The courts should be seen to punish such conduct severely,' said Lord Bingham.

ROADS

A survey by the Refined Bitumen Association (RBA) revealed in April 2000 that compensation to drivers, cyclists and pedestrians for accidents caused by poor roads rose by 50 per cent during 1999 to nearly £1 million a week. I had not realized our roads were that bad; the law, as currently interpreted by the judges, imposes such uncompromisingly strict limits on local councils' legal responsibility for their roads that I would have expected a much lower figure.

Many readers will agree with the comment by Edmund King, executive director of the RAC Foundation: 'Motorists have paid for our roads many times over and deserve a better quality of service.' So what is the legal liability of councils, as local highway authorities, for the roads in their care?

Section 41 of the 1980 Highway Act would seem to be uncompromising in its wording. It states that every authority is 'under a duty to maintain the highway'. Section 58 concedes that in any individual case, it is a defence for an authority to prove that it had taken reasonable care to ensure the highway was not dangerous.

(See also **Icy Roads**). That wonderful word 'reasonable' appears in many statutes and judicial pronouncements, and has always been an essential part of the law's attitude to widely differing problems.

And so – until nearly four years ago – Section 41 was always assumed to exist side by side with the traditional obligation, created by long-standing judge-made law, that we must all in our everyday actions take reasonable care not to cause reasonably foreseeable damage or injury to others. So if a council had not taken reasonable care, in all the circumstances, to maintain a road or make it safe for the public to use, that council would have been liable to pay compensation to anyone who sustained personal injury or loss as a result.

Sadly, that eminently sound principle is – despite the clear wording of the 1980 Act – no longer the law of England. It was killed off by a narrow 3–2 majority decision of five Law Lords in July 1996 in the case of *Stovin* v. *Wise* (*Norfolk County Council, Third Party*). What happened was that Mr Thomas Stovin was driving his motorcycle along a road at Wymondham, Norfolk, at about 1.00 a.m. one Sunday when he collided with a car driven out of a side road into his path by Mrs Rita Wise. Although neither vehicle was travelling at any great speed, Mr Stovin was seriously injured and he sued Mrs Wise for her alleged negligence.

She in turn brought Norfolk County Council into the action as co-defendant, alleging that it was partly to blame in having failed to take effective measures to reduce the risk to road users at what was known to be a dangerous junction.

It transpired that a bank belonging to British Rail on land adjoining the junction obscured road users' views. In fact, three previous accidents had occurred at that very spot. The council knew this and at a meeting with British Rail had acknowledged the visibility problems and recommended removing at least part of the offending bank, provided that BR agreed. Unfortunately, BR did not respond to the council's proposal, despite a further meeting eight months before the accident involving Mr Stovin and Mrs Wise. No further contact between the council and BR took place, and no reminder was sent. The council simply let the matter lie – even though, under Section 79 of the 1980 Act, it could have issued a notice compelling BR to act.

In those circumstances, was the council partly to blame, as Mrs Wise's lawyers maintained, for the eventual accident – i.e., had it failed to take reasonable care to prevent it? Most of us would surely say, 'Undoubtedly, yes!' And that was the ruling of Judge Peter Crawford, QC, in the

High Court, assessing that Mrs Wise was 70 per cent to blame and Norfolk County Council 30 per cent.

Mrs Wise then dropped out of the story and two years later, three judges in the Court of Appeal upheld the judgment against the council. But two years on from then, the House of Lords overruled both Judge Crawford and the Court of Appeal and said the council was legally in no way to blame.

New law was made. In effect, the need for 'reasonable care' by local highway authorities ceased to be the ultimate yardstick of legal responsibility. Lord Hoffman said, speaking for the two other majority Law Lords, 'Drivers must take the highway network as they find it. Everyone knows that there are hazardous bends, intersections and junctions.' Accordingly, local authorities will only be liable for accidents caused by their failure to maintain properly the roads within their area if 'it would in the circumstances have been irrational' – the vital new word – 'not to have exercised the power, so that there was in effect a public duty to act'.

As if that was not enough to make it difficult for road users to sue if a highway authority let them down, Lord Hoffman added that there must also be 'exceptional grounds for holding that the policy of [the 1980 Act] requires compensation to be paid'. In the light of all this, it is quite remarkable that, as the RBA's survey reported, councils are dishing out £1 million a week for accidents caused by defective road maintenance. How is that possible?

The answer is that highway authorities have become

'reactive' rather than 'proactive'. As the RAC's Edmund King has told me, 'They are reacting to accidents that occur rather than having a road maintenance strategy that will prevent accidents happening in the first place.'

I would add that the best way to make the authorities feel so legally vulnerable that they 'react' to accidents is to keep them on their toes by bothering to phone up or write to tell them, every time we see a potential source of danger on the roads: a pothole, a worn or irregular surface, a view-restricting object on adjoining land – whatever. This applies to all road users: motorists, motorcyclists, bicyclists and pedestrians.

The more we tell highway authorities about their failings, the more likely a judge is to hold them to have been 'irrational', to quote Lord Hoffman, in failing to have done anything significant to remedy the situation. This is a positive inducement to complain.

ROADWORTHINESS

It is an offence for anyone, whether a motor trader or a private individual, to sell a motor vehicle 'in an unroadworthy condition', and anyone who uses one on a road in a *dangerous* condition commits an offence against Section 40A of the 1988 Road Traffic Act. The sentence is a maximum £2,500 fine, endorsement with three points and discretionary disqualification. A fixed penalty is available – but only in less serious cases.

Few people use cars that are positively 'dangerous' but many drivers may occasionally be in breach of the 1986 Motor Vehicle (Construction and Use) Regulations. These create a whole variety of maintenance offences, from driving with inefficient brakes to having no water in a windscreen-washer bottle.

As we have already seen under **Random Testing**, the 1988 Act gives a uniformed police officer the right to stop at any time anyone driving a car on a road. If the officer so chooses, he may then spot-check your vehicle's maintenance and, if he finds something wrong, has three options. He can report you for prosecution, give you a fixed penalty notice or hand you a 'vehicle defect form'. This form will specify what is wrong and give you the opportunity of taking the car to a MoT garage to have it put right: if within fourteen days you then produce the form stamped by the garage at a police station, that will be an end of the matter.

The three most serious offences under the 1986 Regulations carry a maximum £2,500 fine, endorsement with three points and discretionary disqualification. They relate to brakes, steering and tyres.

Brakes and steering are straightforward. Every part of the system must be in good working order and if a police officer finds, for instance, excessive travel on the brake pedal or play in the steering, however small, those are offences.

Tyre requirements are, however, more specific. Every tyre must have at least 1.6 mm of tread in a continuous band all the way around the circumference and across 75 per cent of the tread, with *each* defective tyre counting as a separate offence. As for spare tyres, you do not legally have to carry one – but, if you do, its tread must comply with the Regulations.

Most other offences – defective windscreen wipers, windscreens so dirty or cracked that you cannot see through them properly, broken mirrors, faulty exhaust, etc. – attract a lesser maximum fine of £1,000 and no endorsement, penalty points or disqualification. As we have already seen, the fixed penalty system applies.

S

SEAT-BELTS

I suppose that many drivers simply think that a seat-belt is a seat-belt and that both they and their front-seat passengers, of whatever age, must wear one – and leave it at that! In fact, the law is extremely complicated for such an everyday matter.

All cars manufactured since 1965 have to be fitted with adult front seat-belts and all cars manufactured since 1987 must also come with rear seat-belts. In fact, there are still a few older cars legally on the road without front seat-belts and even more without rear seat-belts.

But it has been an offence ever since 1983, with certain exceptions – a driver reversing, anyone with a medical exemption certificate, taxi and minicab drivers, persons riding in a procession (I swear to you that that is a specific exemption!), etc. – for a driver and any passenger aged fourteen or over not to wear a fitted seat-belt when sitting in front – and since 1991 for any passenger not to wear a fitted belt when sitting in the rear.

What about pregnant women – do they have to wear a seat-belt? There is no automatic exemption. They will have to get a medical certificate from their doctor, just like anyone else claiming exemption on medical grounds. In fact, certificates need merely state that it is 'inadvisable on medical grounds' for a person to wear a seat-belt, so a doctor can give a certificate to someone who can wear a seat-belt when it is actually on, but whose physical condition is such that he or she cannot put the belt on or take it off. Doctors are entitled to use their own discretion.

The fixed penalty system applies to seat-belts, so that, if an offence is committed, you can opt to send the local Fixed Penalty Office a £20 fixed penalty in lieu of being taken to court – where the maximum fine that you would be liable to pay under the 1993 Motor Vehicles (Wearing of Seat Belts) Regulations is £500.

Who commits the offence? Drivers are responsible for themselves and for all children under fourteen travelling with them. Otherwise, it is down to every adult passenger – not the driver, as some people believe.

Not wearing a seat-belt can also cost either driver or passenger dearly in a civil court, if suing for damages after an accident caused by another driver's negligence. Back in 1975, even before seat-belt wearing was made compulsory, the Appeal Court ruled that it was obviously so sensible to 'belt up' that not doing so would cut an adult person's damages because of their own 'contributory negligence'.

As Lord Denning laid down, if wearing a seat-belt would have avoided all injury, an adult's damages may be cut by 25 per cent, and by 15 per cent if the injuries would have been 'a good deal less severe'.

The real difficulties about seat-belt law arise when dealing with children. The law is extremely complicated but the basic principle is simple enough: they must always wear appropriate restraints or belts (see **Children**).

SLOW DRIVERS

Is it ever against the law to drive too slowly? The answer is 'Yes'; but it is not going slowly, in itself, which creates an offence. It is the circumstances in which the slow driving occurs.

A hesitant learner driver holding up traffic in a congested town street because he is uncertain at the wheel; the driver of a huge lorry that one cannot pass, an elderly motorist worried about going too fast, a driver of whatever age looking for somewhere to park or who is lost and driving slowly to try and get his bearings, a farm tractor driver on a narrow country road who cannot go any faster: we have met them all.

And they may all be guilty of a variant of careless driving, i.e. driving without reasonable consideration for other road users if they cause unjustified inconvenience to other motorists. In the words of the old song, 'It's not what you do, it's the way that you do it.'

So, for instance, at Wells Magistrates' Court in November 1997, a thirty-three-year-old farm worker who drove a combine harvester at between 5 and 10 miles an hour on the A361 in Somerset on a mid-morning in August and caused a queue of frustrated drivers to build up behind him – including a police motorcyclist! – was fined £120 with £200 costs and had his licence endorsed. The Court Clerk said with some feeling, 'He drove for one and a half miles without stopping to allow a very long queue of traffic to overtake. He could have used the lay-bys to allow the traffic to get by.'

That last remark contains the essence of the law. It is not your slow speed alone that can justify other motorists in reporting you to the police and your being fined up to £2,5000, having your licence endorsed with three to nine penalty points or even (in theory) losing it for a while. It is often your obstinate refusal to let other motorists pass, when it is safe or reasonable for them to do so, that lands you in trouble.

It constitutes no defence in law to believe, however genuinely, 'The world is going too fast. It is the fast drivers who should be arrested, not the slow ones.' That is what a fifty-five-year-old Welsh ex-miner said some years ago after causing a 2-mile tailback within the 30 mph limit on the A473 near Pontypridd by insisting on driving at only 20 miles an hour. The local Bench still fined him £50, ordered him to pay £15 costs and put two penalty points on his licence (before the minimum went up to three).

If you want to drive slowly, you must either choose a road that is appropriate or, on a busy road, do your reasonable best to get out of other people's way.

Paragraph 145 of the Highway Code clearly lays down: 'Do not hold up a long queue of traffic, especially if you are driving a large or slow-moving vehicle. Check your mirrors frequently, and if necessary pull in where it is safe and let traffic pass.'

Depending on the circumstances, it is not slow drivers who need fear the law but selfish ones.

SPEEDING

This is the one offence which most motorists commit. DETR figures indicate that about 70 per cent of all drivers exceed the 30 mph limit (let alone the others!), despite the increasing presence of speed cameras and improved warning signs. Most of us, no doubt, like to think that we only exceed the permitted limit 'within reason'. But there is *never* a legal excuse for doing so, except when driving a vehicle for fire brigade, ambulance or police purposes (see **Police Cars and Other Emergency Service Vehicles**).

The rest of us, when caught, can only throw ourselves on the mercy of the police officer who has stopped us. A lot depends on the individual officer and on your own attitude. Politeness usually pays dividends.

In practice, whatever the official guidelines by the Association of Chief Police Officers (ACPO) may say (see **Zero Tolerance**), I have a sneaking suspicion that the old rule of thumb once given me by a senior police officer still operates: that the usual 'starting-point' for police action is only reached when the relevant limit is exceeded by '10 per cent plus 2'. For instance, within a 30-mph built-up area, you will generally only be stopped if you are travelling at more than 35 mph: i.e. 30 plus 3 (10 per cent of 30) plus 2.

Thereafter, a kind of sliding scale applies. If you exceed the relevant limit by up to 10 mph, you will probably only get a warning for future behaviour. If you are 10–25 mph over the limit, you can usually expect to be offered a £40 fixed penalty – *which, as a general rule, you should accept*. It will cost much less than going to court: £40 and three penalty points as against a fine of up to £1,000 (or £2,500, if speeding on a motorway), and your licence endorsed with three to six penalty points. Only if you have exceeded the relevant limit by more than 25 mph will you usually not be offered a fixed penalty but taken to court.

What are the limits? Unless official signs show otherwise, they are 30 mph on 'restricted roads': i.e. roads in built-up areas in England and Wales with street lamps not more than 185 metres (200 yards) apart (Class C and unclassified roads in Scotland with lamps not more than 185 metres (200 yards apart), 60 mph on single carriageways and 70 mph on dual carriageways and motorways. And if you are towing a caravan or trailer, those last two limits are lowered by 10 mph – which not everyone remembers!

But you should always remember that the speed limit alone is not the sole criterion. As Rule 104 of the Highway Code spells out, 'The speed limit is the absolute maximum and does not mean it is safe to drive at that speed irrespective of conditions.' Rule 124 repeats the message: 'Do not treat speed limits as a target. It is often not appropriate or safe to drive at the maximum speed limit. Take the road and traffic conditions into account . . . Be prepared to adjust your speed as a precaution.'

If not, you are liable to be stopped and booked for careless driving, at the very least.

STOLEN CAR

If your car is stolen, can there be legal hassles about retrieving it? This question is of more than academic interest to over half a million drivers annually. According to the AA, a car crime is committed every twenty seconds in Britain: either the car itself is stolen or something is taken from it.

If the car is found abandoned or unharmed, there is rarely a problem about getting it back. You will have told the police that it is missing and they will tell you to which police pound it was taken. But sometimes the car will have been sold and then complications can set in. The governing legal principle is expressed in Latin: *Nemo dat quod non habet* ('Nobody can give what he does not have'). So the thief cannot give good title to the car to anyone he sells it to. He cannot give what he does not have – whether or not the so-called purchaser knows or suspects that the car is stolen.

The purchaser's state of mind does not come into it as far as the civil law of ownership is concerned. If the police can prove he knew the car was stolen, they can charge him with dishonestly handling stolen goods and he can be jailed or fined.

But, irrespective of the criminal law, even if the would-be purchaser 'bought' the car in good faith, he still gets no legal title and the rightful owner can instantly reclaim the vehicle. What about the motorist who has paid out good money for a 'bent' car? His only legal remedy is to sue the person who 'sold' it to him – if he can find him and he is worth suing.

I say that the rightful owner can instantly reclaim his vehicle. But, in April 1993, one motorist in Greater Manchester opted to buy back her stolen car from its new 'owner' when police warned that she could be arrested if she drove it home. Her beige C-registration Ford Sierra, which she had bought the previous summer for £1,200, was taken from outside her home and, by the time it turned up a week later, it had been snapped up by a new 'owner' for £400. He did not know it was stolen. He had 'bought' it in good faith.

But the local police would not let the woman drive it away. 'I was told that if we attempted to take the car back, we would be arrested for theft,' she said. So, faced with a lengthy legal battle, she agreed to buy back her own car for £120! A detective on Greater Manchester's stolen vehicle squad commented, 'It's a classic car-theft scenario. She still had the title to the car but could be arrested for theft if she took it away. The man who bought it in good faith was not allowed to drive it because it was stolen.' Is that the legal position? For the so-called purchaser, yes. Once he knew the car was stolen, he could no longer drive it legally. But as regards the vehicle's true owner, the Greater Manchester police seem to have taken a highly technical view of the law.

Undoubtedly, Section 1 of the 1968 Theft Act states, 'A person is guilty of theft if he dishonestly appropriates property belonging to another with the intention of permanently depriving the other of it,' and Section 5 defines 'belonging to another' as 'belonging to any person having possession or control of it or having in it any proprietary right or interest'. So it would seem that the local police believed that the car belonged both to the original owner, who had a proprietary right in the vehicle, and to the purchaser, who was the person having possession or control of it, and were happy to let the civil courts sort it out. I am sure they were mistaken, and an AA spokesman assures me that he knows of no similar case. He called it 'staggering'. So, before you rush into any deal with the 'new owner' of your stolen car, check with the highest-ranking local police officer available and, if you are still not satisfied, consult a solicitor or a citizens' advice bureau.

STOPPING ON A ROAD AT NIGHT

This is different from parking in the daytime, which we have already looked at under **Parking.** Special rules apply when you leave your vehicle on a road at night:

The car must be facing the direction of the traffic flow except when left in 'a recognized parking space', which means on a meter or in a resident's parking bay – even though it is outside 'normal hours' (Regulation 101 of the 1986 Road Vehicles (Construction and Use Regulations) and Regulation 24 of the 1989 Road Vehicles Lighting Regulations).

The car must display parking lights when left on a road or in a lay-by on a road with a speed limit greater than 30 mph (Regulation 24 of the 1989 Regulations).

Cars, goods vehicles not exceeding 1525 kg (1½ tons) unladen, invalid carriages and motorcycles may be left without lights on a road (or in a lay-by) with a speed limit of 30 mph or less if they are at least 10 metres (32 feet) away from any junction, close to the kerb and facing in the direction of the traffic flow or in a recognized parking place or lay-by (Regulation 24 of the 1989 Regulations).

T

TAX DISC

In legal jargon, a tax disc is a 'current vehicle excise licence'. Regulation 16 of the 1971 Road Vehicles (Registration and Licensing) Regulations says that this annual licence must be displayed on the nearside windscreen of all four-wheeled motor vehicles while they are in use or kept on a public road. The disc must be clearly visible in daylight from the pavement, as readily observable proof that the current vehicle excise duty – what everyone calls 'road tax' – has been paid. Motorcycles must display the disc on the nearside in front of the driving seat.

The obligation to pay road tax arises, under the 1994 Vehicle Excise and Registration Act, whenever a motor vehicle is on a public road, even if it has broken down or is not in use. If you fail to display a current tax disc *in the proper place on the windscreen*, your vehicle may be wheel-clamped and you can be fined up to £200. If you have not paid the road tax, you face an additional penalty of up to £1,000 or five times the annual rate of duty payable, whichever is the greater.

If you have had a current tax disc at any time since 31 January 1998 but decide that you do not wish to tax your vehicle any more because you will no longer be using or keeping it on a public road, you must declare this to the DVLA. You can either do this on your vehicle licence renewal reminder form that the DVLA will automatically send you as your current licence nears its expiry date or you can declare a Statutory Off Road Notification (SORN) using a form that you can obtain from the DVLA Customer Enquiry Unit (tel. 01792 772 134). If you fail to make a SORN declaration when you should, you may be fined up to £1,000. The declaration will be valid for twelve months unless you relicense, sell, permanently export or scrap the vehicle before that time has expired. The DVLA will normally send you a reminder form when the declaration is about to expire. Motorists sometimes get themselves into trouble by transferring their current tax disc from one vehicle to another. This is not only stupid but seriously criminal, amounting to fraudulent use of the disc. The 1994 Act specifies a fine of up to £5,000 and/or a maximum of two years in jail.

You must apply for a new disc in time to replace the old one as soon as it expires. The widespread belief that there is a fourteen-day period of grace is a myth. Telling a police officer that you have already applied for a new disc but it has not yet come through is technically no defence – even if true – but it may help you escape without a prosecution. As so often, it depends on how polite you are!

Finally, cars constructed before 1 January 1973 are exempt from duty. There is *some* virtue in having an old car.

TOTTING UP

This has been with us since November 1982 when the 1981
Transport Act came into effect. It is intended to be simple
for drivers to understand and for magistrates to enforce.
And so it is. There can hardly be a driver in the land who
does not know that if you commit an endorsable offence
which 'tots up' to twelve or more penalty points incurred
for other offences over the past three years, a court *must*
disqualify you for at least six months unless there are
strong mitigating circumstances. This procedure applies
irrespective of how serious – or not – your most recent
offence may be. Even though it may merit only three
penalty points, if that brings your total for the past three
years to twelve points or more, you will be banned for at
least six months, unless a court considers there are strong
mitigating circumstances – which seldom happens.

Furthermore, if all the previous offences were for speeding, the greatest potential source of death on our roads, it
makes the prospect of minimum disqualification almost
inevitable. So when, in 1998, ex-Formula One world cham-
pion Nigel Mansell was caught travelling at 92 mph on a
70-mph dual carriageway in his new £233,000 turbo-
charged Bentley Continental (he said the car was so well
sound-proofed that he did not realize his speed), and
magistrates at Yeovil, Somerset handed down five points
which, together with nine points for two previous speeding
offences, brought his three-year total to fourteen, his lawyer told the Bench: 'He does not seek to waste the court's

time in arguing that he should not be disqualified.' She concentrated on persuading the Bench to limit disqualification to the minimum six months, and was perhaps somewhat fortunate in achieving her aim.

So many people may well have wondered how famous footballer and clothes-prop David Beckham managed to keep his licence in December 1999 and get quashed on appeal Stockport magistrates' eight-month ban based on 'totting up'. You may remember that he had been caught speeding at 76 mph in his £150,000 Ferrari Maranello on a 50-mph bypass when he already had ten points on his licence for *three* earlier speeding offences within the previous three years. He claimed that he had been forced to break the speed limit because he was being hounded by a paparazzo photographer in a Ford Fiesta who had followed him for 10 miles – but was never apprehended. Mr Nigel Flynn, the Chairman of the Bench, told Mr Beckham: 'We find that there are no special reasons in this case. We consider that there were alternative courses of action open to you other than exceeding the speed limit by 26 mph.'

But a week later at Manchester's Minshull Street Crown Court, it was a very different story. This time, Judge Barry Woodward told Mr Beckham: 'We are satisfied these facts do constitute special reasons and we [he was sitting with two local magistrates] are going to allow the appeal against sentencing to the extent of not endorsing Mr Beckham's licence.' This meant that David Beckham's fourth speeding conviction stood but there was no endorsement, therefore no penalty points which go automatically with an endorsement – and his tally remained at only ten, safely within the disqualification threshold.

How was this possible? What was all this mumbo-jumbo about 'special reasons'?

The answer will be of interest to many ordinary motorists, not merely high-profile young footballers.

One has to go back to first principles. Section 35 (4) of the 1988 Road Traffic Offenders Act states that 'totting-up' magistrates must ban drivers over the twelve-point threshold for at least six months 'unless satisfied, having regard to all the circumstances, that there are grounds mitigating the normal consequences of the conviction'. That is not easy to establish. Under the old law before the Act, you could always plead personal hardship: for example, you would lose your job if disqualified, or an innocent person would suffer, such as an elderly relative dependent on you for transport.

The result was that too many frequent offenders kept their licence. So the 1988 Act specified that only *exceptional* hardship should be taken into account. In 1996, when a taxi driver in Scotland (where the law is the same as in England) claimed that losing his licence would probably mean losing his job, the High Court of Justiciary ruled that, although that would be hardship, it would not be 'exceptional hardship'.

So, in recent years, experienced defence lawyers' emphasis has moved from seeking to persuade magistrates that they should not disqualify a motorist for having accumulated more than twelve points, to not endorsing any – or fewer than to be expected – points for the latest offence so that disqualification does not arise: their client remains safely within the 'totting-up' threshold.

This ploy is tried every day of the week – with varying degrees of success – in magistrates' courts up and down the country. In David Beckham's case, on appeal, it won hands down.

Since he was only two points short of the threshold and the lowest possible number of points that can be awarded for speeding is three (six is the maximum), this meant that his lawyer had to argue that there should be no endorsement at all so that there was no possibility of penalty points.

The legal criterion for not endorsing is different from not disqualifying in 'totting-up' cases. The 1988 Road Traffic Offenders Act calls it 'special reasons', and the High Court has laid down that there must be something 'special' about the circumstances of the driving and not merely about the driver himself. On this basis, it was irrelevant that David Beckham was the sort of driver who had already been caught speeding three times within the last three years. So Judge Woodward could rule: 'Reasonably fearing there could be a 50-mph crash on a relatively busy dual carriageway, Mr Beckham decided to exceed the speed limit over a relatively short distance in a burst of speed for the purpose of putting distance between him and his pursuer.'

Lucky chap. If, indeed, there is the same law for celebrities and the rest of us, which I sometimes doubt, this means that any potential 'totter' should endeavour to put the best possible light on his latest misdemeanour. 'I didn't really mean to do it, I had to' is an argument that can, perhaps with a vivid imagination, be applied to a whole range of circumstances.

TOWING AWAY AND CLAMPING

A fine or fixed penalty charge is not the only possible consequence of illegal parking. There are also the twin curses of a modern motorist's life: towing away and (so far only in London), clamping.

(See also **Private Clamping**). Besides the inconvenience (and often the cost of a taxi to the car pound), towing away costs a £105 release fee plus storage charges if you do not collect your car from the pound on the same day, *and* there is the parking fine or penalty charge on top of that. Clamping costs a £100 declamping fee plus the penalty charge.

Section 99 of the 1984 Road Traffic Regulation Act gives general authority for cars to be towed away when 'illegally, obstructively or dangerously parked'. This is *supposed* to happen only when cars are parked 'obstructively or dangerously' but, in practice, many motorists would agree that cars merely parked illegally are also towed away.

The actual towing away is generally done by private firms operating at a profit. They need the prior authority of a police officer, traffic warden or parking attendant, but some of us suspect that their role may sometimes have as much to do with money-earning as with law enforcement. Contrary to popular belief, clamping is not restricted to vehicles parked dangerously or for a long time. Like many other motorists in London, I have seen Post Office vans, delivery vans and even taxis clamped. In one case, a man's car was clamped while he was inside it sleeping!

The legal basis is that the 1984 Road Traffic Regulation Act enables a police officer or traffic warden to authorize clamping when *any* parking law is infringed. London parking attendants have an even freer hand: the only legal restraint imposed by the 1991 Road Traffic Act is that vehicles on a meter cannot be clamped unless they have overstayed for at least fifteen minutes.

TRAFFIC LIGHTS

For a start, what do traffic lights actually mean? Red alone is a legal command to 'Stop', and you must wait behind the line marked on the road. Red and amber also mean 'Stop', and you must not pass through or start until green shows. Amber alone means 'Stop', and you may drive on only if the light appears after you have crossed the stop line or are so close to it that to pull up might cause an accident.

Green means you that may drive on – but only if the road is clear. It is not a command to continue. You should treat its invitation to proceed with caution. As the Highway Code advises, 'Take special care if you intend to turn left or right and give way to pedestrians who are crossing.' Regulation 33(2) of the 1994 Traffic Signs Regulations and

General Directions, in fact, spells out that when traffic lights say you can proceed, you should only do so 'with due regard to the safety of other road users'.

And, of course, do not 'jump' the lights. That could lead not only to a charge of failing to obey traffic lights, which carries a maximum fine of £1,000 and three penalty points, although the fixed-penalty system applies, but also to the more serious charge of careless driving with a maximum fine of £2,500 and three to nine penalty points – with no fixed penalty.

Four common situations are of interest.

The traffic lights do not work

If you disobey an official set of traffic lights, whether they are working properly or not, you commit an offence against the 1994 Traffic Signs Regulations and General Directions. If the lights are jammed at red, you must either turn round and find another outlet or else stop – and remain stopped until a police officer or traffic warden comes along and countermands the red light by beckoning you forward.

However, a judge commented many years ago in a case at Hertford Quarter Sessions (the equivalent of a present-day Crown Court) that, if a motorist were to edge forward carefully without causing damage or injury, the appropriate sentence would usually be only an absolute discharge – which does not count as a conviction. So, in practice, a police officer should only give you a polite warning.

But if the lights fail completely and show no colour whatsoever, the legal position is different. You can treat the junction as uncontrolled and you commit no offence, even technically, in carefully proceeding.

Temporary traffic lights at road works and traffic-control schemes

A reader once wrote to me: 'Concerning temporary traffic lights, I would like to know the Act of Parliament which allows a road repairer or hole digger the right to erect traffic lights and have the full backing of our Parliament regardless of any qualification.' In fact, the position is not so chaotic as that. A man cannot simply come along and dig a hole in the road as the whim takes him.

Section 14 of the 1984 Road Traffic Regulation Act gives the local council, acting as traffic authority, the right to order temporary traffic restrictions for up to eighteen months, subject to six months' extension, in certain specified circumstances. These are to enable works to be done on or near roads, to avoid danger to the public or serious damage to roads unrelated to roadworks, or to facilitate street cleaning and litter removal. Section 9 of the same Act also allows similar temporary orders to be made for 'experimental' traffic schemes.

But traffic authorities are not given a free hand to do exactly as they like. Section 122 imposes upon them an over-all duty to have regard to the desirability of maintaining reasonable access to neighbouring premises. Furthermore, courts strictly construe the wording of Sections 9 and 14: for instance, in April 1996, the High Court ruled that it was unlawful for West Lancashire District Council to use the power to make an order 'for the purpose of

carrying out an experimental scheme of traffic control'
where the real purpose was to ban for eighteen months
heavy goods vehicles from using an access road to a neighbouring landfill site. That was not an 'experiment' but a
simple prohibition.

What is the legal status of temporary traffic lights? Some
motorists believe that, even when they are showing red,
you do not have to stop if you can safely see your way
ahead. That is simply not so. The 1994 Regulations give
them equal validity with permanent traffic lights. If they
show red, you must stop – even if the way ahead is clear.

But all this is criminal law where the police may be
involved. One final question remains: what about civil law
where the only issue is whether you can sue or be sued by
another private citizen for damages in the event of an
accident?

In *Eva (Joseph) Ltd* v. *Reeves*, as far back as 1938, the law
was laid down in uncompromising terms that a driver with
a green light in his favour owes no duty to traffic entering
a crossing in disobedience to the lights – except that, if he
actually sees such traffic, he must take all reasonable steps
to avoid a collision. In other words, although many prudent motorists look to see if anyone is, for whatever reason,
going to disobey the lights, they are unlikely to be held
guilty of contributory negligence for failing to do so.

So, for instance, when a motorist with his right indicator
flashing moved off from stationary to turn right when
traffic lights changed in his favour and a car approaching
at 45 mph from the opposite direction with the lights at
red could not stop and smashed into him, a judge ruled

that the motorist turning right was 10 per cent contributorily negligent and accordingly reduced his damages by a tenth. But the Appeal Court overruled him and said that the driver was entitled to assume he was visible to the other motorist and that it was safe to cross when he did.

TYRES

As we have already seen under **Roadworthiness**, Regulation 27 of the 1986 Road Vehicles (Construction and Use) Regulations states that every car tyre must have at least 1.6 mm of tread in a continuous band all the way around the circumference and across 75 per cent of the tread, with *each* defective tyre counting as a separate offence. How likely are you to be prosecuted for this offence – which carries a maximum fine of £2,500?

Unless you are unlucky enough to be involved in an accident to which the police are called, you are not really at much risk. Only a particularly zealous police officer is likely to report you for a breach of Regulation 27 merely because he happens to notice on his beat that one or other of the tyres on your parked car has less than the prescribed tread. But once you have an accident, all this changes: not only are you likely to face a prosecution if the police are called but, even if the police are not involved, the state of your tyres will be a crucial factor in assessing whether you have been negligent so as to have to pay compensation in a civil court. Irrespective of the 1986 Regulations which make criminal law, every prudent motorist is supposed to ensure that his tyres are properly inflated and with a tread that is not a potential danger to himself or other road users.

Incidentally, the Regulations also make it an offence to drive with tyres that are not properly inflated. What about a spare tyre? Surprisingly, you do not legally have to carry one – but, if you do, *and use it*, its tread must also comply with the Regulations.

As for motorcycles, their tyres must have at least 1.0 mm of tread in a continuous band, etc. whereas mopeds – presumably because they are so much lighter – need only have a tread that is 'visible'.

U

USED CARS

Formerly, used cars were called 'secondhand cars' but, in this PR-conscious age, the term 'used car' somehow does not sound so tacky or down-market. 'Secondhand car' sounds less like something you could have bought off dear old, slightly 'bent' Arthur Daley. But has the law kept pace with this upgrading? The answer is 'Yes'. Buying a car which has had at least one previous owner is no longer so much of a legal hazard as it once was – at least, if you buy it from a dealer.

Both dealers and private sellers commit an offence against Section 75 of the 1988 Road Traffic Act if they sell an unroadworthy car. Under the 1979 Sale of Goods Act, both must sell a vehicle that is theirs to sell and not one that has been stolen or that belongs to a finance company under a hire purchase agreement, and both must sell a car that corresponds with their description.

For instance, back in 1967, a motorist in Welwyn Garden City, Hertfordshire, advertised a 1961 Triumph Herald for sale. Unfortunately, unknown to him, it was an amalgam of two Triumph Heralds. A previous owner had put together the back of a 1961 model with the front of an older one. The Appeal Court ruled that the vehicle was not 'a 1961 Triumph Herald' and awarded the buyer damages.

But, in two important respects, your rights are much stronger if you buy from a dealer and not from a private individual. Section 3 of the 1968 Trade Descriptions Act and Section 14 of the 1979 Sale of Goods Act apply only to persons selling goods, whether new or used, 'in the course of a trade or business'. Private sales are not affected: *Caveat emptor*, 'Let the Buyer Beware!' still prevails.

This has two major consequences for dealers' sales.

In the realm of criminal law, a dealer risks a fine and even going to jail under the 1968 Act if he sells a car with a 'false trade description'.

According to Professor Brian Harvey of Birmingham University, 'clocking' (where the milometer is fraudulently turned back) 'is probably the most persistent offence under the 1968 Act'. As long ago as 1978, the then Director General of Fair Trading stated that in the course of making 1,614 routine checks, over 50 per cent of vehicles were found to have been 'clocked', costing purchasers an estimated £50 million a year.

Yet for nearly twenty years, it was generally believed that a dealer could escape liability for 'clocking' by sticking a disclaimer on the milometer saying its reading was not guaranteed or by saying so in his invoices or in a prominently displayed notice. It was not until June 1987 that Lord Lane, then Lord Chief Justice, ruled in *R. v. Southwood* that a dealer who has himself tampered with the milometer can never hide behind a disclaimer. The law – belatedly – was not so stupid. Only a dealer who has mistakenly or carelessly accepted a false reading from a previous owner *may* escape conviction with 'a bold, precise and compelling' disclaimer.

The other popular kind of dealer's 'false trade description' is the lying over-sell: whether written or merely oral. But the courts have been astute to curb excess.

For instance, 'showroom condition throughout' refers not only to a car's external appearance but also to its interior and mechanical condition, so that a Portsmouth dealer was fined for using this phrase when advertising a car with a defective engine. Also successful prosecutions have established that 'in excellent condition throughout' – another well-used forecourt phrase – is nonsense when the car does not run properly. As *Stone's Justices' Manual*, the magistrates' bible, states: 'It is no answer to say that the car is in as good a condition as would be expected of an unrepaired car of its age and mileage. If repairs are needed, it will not be "excellent" until they are carried out.'

In the realm of civil law, under the 1979 Sale of Goods Act, as amended in 1994, the car must be of 'satisfactory quality'. This means that – apart from defects which were obvious or pointed out before purchase – if things go wrong within a reasonably short time, whether or not you road-tested the vehicle before buying it, you can give it back and reclaim the purchase price. You should stop using the car at once and tell the dealer immediately, confirming any oral complaint in writing.

'Satisfactory quality' is a lower standard than 'merchantable quality', which appeared in the Act before the 1994 amendment. In the old days, you often lost the right to reject the vehicle if you agreed to repairs which then failed to rectify the fault. You were deemed to have 'accepted' the car in its original state and could no longer reject it but had to be content with damages or a partial refund. Each case depends on its own facts. But nowadays judges are much more likely to rule that you can insist on giving back an 'unsatisfactory' car, even if you have tried to be reasonable and allowed the dealer to try to repair it.

U-TURN

You have to be careful where you choose to do this. Making a U-turn on a road when there is an official traffic sign saying 'No U-turns' constitutes the offence of disobeying the sign, contrary to Regulation 10 of the 1994 Traffic Signs and Regulations and General Directions. But apart from this specific offence, you must always take special care because, if your manoeuvre causes an accident, you would almost certainly be liable to compensate anyone injured and local magistrates could also find you guilty of careless driving.

Making a U-turn on a motorway is always an offence against the 1982 Motorways Traffic (England and Wales) Regulations – except when done under the authority of a police officer, usually in the case of a major traffic jam ahead

(See also **Motorways**).

V

VEHICLE RECALL

This is when a manufacturer advertises in the press or otherwise gets in touch with car owners telling them to bring back a particular model for checks because a design fault or production defect has been discovered. In 2000 in the United States, for example, Ford was forced by law to recall thousands of Explorers with Bridgestone tyres, because they were blamed for causing almost 1,500 accidents – although fortunately Fords in Britain were not affected.

In this country, the safety recall system is voluntary. Car makers are under no legal duty to recall vehicles for repairs to safety systems such as brakes and steering. But the Vehicle Inspectorate (VI), the Government body that administers the British car makers' safety recall scheme, maintains that British car owners – and their passengers – are not at risk. It says that our car makers declare about 90 per cent of safety problems and it hears about the rest from routine MoT tests.

How does our system work? When a car maker becomes aware of a safety defect experienced by many cars of a specific model and posing a significant risk to the public, it tells the VI which then issues a general recall notice and gives the car maker access to the DVLA's records so that it can contact its customers. It also writes to the registered owners of these vehicles inviting them to have their car checked at their nearest brand dealer. If there is no response, a second letter is sent by recorded delivery. In fact, the system works surprisingly well: about 85 per cent of cars wanted for recall are traced and checked, compared with only 65 per cent in America.

VITAL LEGAL TERMS

It may help to discuss briefly three of the most common legal terms that I have used without explanation in the preceding entries, as follows.

Fine

All motoring offences carry maximum fines which are at five distinct levels: £200, £500, £1,000, £2,500 or £5,000. These are the amounts 'up to' which a court can order a defendant to pay. They are Parliament's way of showing its view of the seriousness of that type of offence, but the actual amount in any particular case will depend on its own specific facts and will generally be much less than the maximum, especially with a first or infrequent offender.

Licence endorsement

If you are convicted of anything except the most minor offence, the court, in accordance with the 1988 Road Traffic

Offenders Act, must order the facts of the conviction and sentence to be 'endorsed' – i.e. written – on your licence. The idea is to create an instantly available record so that any police officer – or magistrate – looking at your licence in the future can immediately see your legal track record.

'Special reasons'

A court can decide not to endorse (and even, with a major offence, not to disqualify), if you can persuade it that 'special reasons' exist. You will have to attend court and give evidence and, as we saw under **Court Cases**, probably engage a lawyer to speak for you, even if pleading guilty. It is usually an uphill task. As the High Court ruled fifty years ago, 'the reasons must be special to the offence and not to the offender'.

You cannot, for instance, argue that your personal circumstances are 'special': that you would lose your job if your licence were endorsed or you were disqualified. Tough! There must be something 'special' about the circumstances of the actual offence, such as you were speeding your heavily pregnant wife to hospital in an emergency when no other transport was available.

W

WARNING LIGHTS

These are supposed to warn other road users that your vehicle is, for whatever reason, causing a temporary hazard. Regulation 27 of the 1989 Road Vehicle Lighting Regulations specifies in surprising detail when it is an offence to switch warning lights on: i.e. 'other than (i) to warn persons using the road of a temporary obstruction when the vehicle is at rest; or (ii) on a motorway or unrestricted dual carriageway, to warn following drivers of a need to slow down due to a temporary obstruction ahead; or (iii) in the case of a bus, to summon assistance for the driver or any person acting as a conductor or inspector of the vehicle; or (iv) in the case of a bus to which prescribed signs are fitted, when the vehicle is stationary and children under the age of sixteen years are entering or leaving, or are about to enter or leave, or have just left the vehicle.'

I have quoted that piece of legalese in full to give you some idea of how complicated and turgid the actual sources of motoring law can be.

WINDSCREEN CLEANERS

Aggressive windscreen cleaners at traffic lights are a curse for motorists. How does the law treat them? In nothing like so tough a way as it treats the long-suffering motorist. As so often today in modern Britain, one is left wondering who really is the criminal.

I ask you to consider this court case in Brighton in July 1993. The thirty-year-old owner of a BMW was in the driving seat, his car having stopped at traffic lights. A burly youth approached him and started wiping his windscreen without saying anything. The driver ignored him, but the youth put his head inside the car and swore at him. As the driver later explained, 'If someone puts their head in my car window and shouts threats at me I am going to defend myself, and that is what I did. I got out and grabbed hold of the washer boy. It was a push rather than a slap. His glasses fell off and broke. I offered to pay for them. Within fifteen minutes I went to a police box and reported what had happened.'

What happened next? No prizes for guessing that it was the motorist, not the foul-mouthed washer boy, who ended up at Brighton Magistrates' Court charged with disorderly behaviour, contrary to the 1986 Public Order Act. In fact, the magistrates threw out the case without the motorist even being called to give evidence, and awarded him £300 costs. The motorist said the case was 'a disgraceful waste of public money' and was congratulated on his acquittal by his local MP, then Solicitor General Sir Derek Spencer.

Sir Derek said that aggressive windscreen cleaners 'are the bane of Brighton. You feel under threat if you don't accede to their request.'

But the truly significant comment was made by a local police inspector: 'We get complaints about washer boys, but criminal law does not cover that area.' That is absolute nonsense, and yet one more example of how the police today are vigilant to protect the wrong people, the law breakers instead of the law abiders.

A cheery request – 'Want your windscreen cleaned, mate?' – before the cleaner swoops across the window is not a crime as most people would use that term. None the less there have been several cases in London in which non-intimidating windscreen cleaners have been convicted of street trading without a licence.

On the other hand, aggressive cleaners commit, at the very least, the very offence with which the unfortunate Brighton motorist was charged: namely, 'using threatening, abusive or insulting words or behaviour or disorderly behaviour within the hearing or sight of a person likely to be caused harassment, alarm or distress thereby', contrary to Section 5 of the 1986 Act. If convicted, they can be fined up to £1,000.

But they are getting away with it in many other places than Brighton. What on earth are the police and the Crown Prosecution Service playing at? Why are they so timid in their enforcement of the law? Busy road junctions are being polluted by this breed of modern highwayman extorting money from their victims with threats implicit in their very manner. Holding the windscreen squeegee aloft in an aggressive fashion or starting to clean the window before the motorist agrees can easily, even without foul language, be interpreted by a court as 'threatening behaviour' within the meaning of Section 4 of the 1986 Act.

The use of foul language can easily bring perpetrators within Section 5 of the same Act, which is a much tougher proposition. It penalizes the use of 'threatening, abusive or insulting words or behaviour with intent to cause a person to believe that immediate unlawful violence will be used against him'. And it lays down a maximum sentence of six months in jail and/or a £2,500 fine.

But prosecutions under either Section 4 or Section 5 of the 1986 Act are few and far between.

WINTER DRIVING

The natural hazards of winter driving are obvious: ice, snow, rain, fog, frost and flooding. But there are also considerable legal hazards. It was back in 1954 that Lord Justice Somervell said, 'This danger of slippery or icy surfaces is an incident of the winter in our country which everyone encounters and it is something one must anticipate and deal with oneself.'

To some extent, the law has moved on since then and motorists involved in accidents because of adverse weather conditions have won damages from local authorities who have failed to take reasonable care to maintain their roads in a safe condition. But, as we have seen in **Roads**, it has been an uphill struggle that is still going on, fought out against the background of the stern judicial philosophy formulated all those years ago by the late Sir Donald Somervell.

To be fair, Somervell's way of thinking applies throughout the whole spectrum of normal everyday activity: from factory workers slipping on an icy patch going to work first thing in the morning despite their employers' efforts to keep the entrance sanded; to train commuters slipping on icy platforms that have only just been sanded and salted; to motorists coping with thunderstorms, cloudbursts and ice. The underlying principle is that you cannot use bad weather as an excuse, if you are a motorist, for your own bad – or inconsiderate – driving.

Indeed, it has been undisputed law in England since an Appeal Court decision in 1960 that there is not even a legal duty on highway authorities to warn motorists of icy patches on the roads or 'black ice ahead'. Three Lords Justices said that the authorities could do so if they wished, but they were under no legal obligation. You have to keep your eyes open on wintry roads and be alert to possible dangers without necessarily being given any warning (see **Icy Roads**).

Section 41 of the 1980 Highway Act *does* impose on local highway authorities the legal duty to maintain the roads within their area and the courts have ruled that 'maintain' is wider than a mere duty to keep in repair and may oblige an authority to pre-salt roads when they know that frost is imminent or to grit or clear roads after snow has fallen. Even so, Section 58 of the Act says that it is a defence that a highway authority 'has taken such care as in all the circumstances was reasonable'.

With limited resources, there is no absolute guarantee of the safety of any of our roads – at any time.

Even when the courts are prepared to rule that a highway authority has, in the specific circumstances, failed in its legal duty, that still does not give the driver (or his insurance company) cast-iron protection in the event of an accident. For instance, one September evening in the Midlands after it had been pouring all day – and it was not yet even winter! – a motorist drove into a pool of water that had collected across the road and shot across the asphalt surface straight into an oncoming car. He was killed outright and the people in the other car were badly injured. The surviving driver, backed by his insurance company, sued the dead driver's executors and the local highway authority for damages. Why the authority? Because it was alleged, and proved, that, although they knew that particular stretch of road always flooded after rain, they had done nothing whatsoever to remedy the situation. They could have altered the camber of the road or improved the drainage but they had chosen to do neither.

Eventually, the Appeal Court ruled that they were primarily responsible for the accident. But the dead motorist's executors still had to pay one-third of the damages: 'He must have been driving far too fast in the conditions then prevailing,' said Lord Denning, then Master of the Rolls. He was therefore ruled to have been one-third to blame because of his 'contributory negligence'.

One may feel the decision was rather harsh but one has

to remember that the surviving driver's speed in his Jaguar was only 25 mph against the other's near-70 mph. As Lord Denning commented, 'On that night no one should have done any more than 25 mph.'

And the fact that the dead driver's car had obviously gone into a skid before crashing into the Jaguar did not help his case at all. One cannot say, 'I skidded. Therefore, I am not to blame.' As Mr Justice MacKenna ruled in another case: 'An unexplained and violent skid is, *in itself*, evidence of negligence.' The comment was made in the High Court following an incident on a cold, wet November night on a rain-slashed road in Surrey. A man was driving his Bentley when, as he said, 'suddenly it went into a violent skid and I found myself facing the other way on the other side of the road. A couple of seconds later I felt a violent bang' – when an oncoming car crashed into him.

He could not explain his car's skid. He claimed his foot had not touched the brake pedal. He had done nothing to cause the accident. So could he blame it all on the atrocious weather conditions? 'No,' ruled Mr Justice MacKenna. The fact that he had skidded for no apparent reason was in itself enough to saddle him with liability.

The prospect of success in court with regard to winter driving mishaps is often difficult to assess. It must be admitted that some motorists drive without proper regard to prevailing weather conditions, travelling at speeds and in a manner that would be dangerous even if the sun were shining down from untroubled skies. They – and all of us – should ponder what Lord Greene said in the Appeal Court over fifty years ago: 'If roads are in such a condition that a motor car cannot safely proceed at all, it is the driver's duty to stop. If the roads are in such a condition that it is not safe to go at more than a foot's pace, his duty is to proceed at a foot's pace.'

I cannot put it more clearly.

X

EXCUSES

Excuses, excuses – when will they help a motorist in court? Only in comparatively rare circumstances; and then the story has to be really good – as happened years ago when my old friend Sir Stirling Moss got a parking summons on going to bring his then wife home from a London hospital where she had just given birth to their baby daughter. He claimed he was using his car as an ambulance – and got the case thrown out. There is also the marvellous story of an Ipswich sculptor who, when given a parking ticket, said to the traffic warden, 'I have a rhinoceros with me – did you expect me to carry it?' Subsequently he produced the 30-pound steel rhinoceros model in court – and he too got an acquittal.

But sadly there are many more cases that end with a conviction. Consider, for instance, the plight of the nineteen-year-old London postman who in February 1993 became the first driver to be convicted by police roadside speed-trap cameras. He admitted to the Ealing magistrates that he had been driving at 78 mph on the 50-mph-limit A40, but explained he was hurrying to see his pregnant ex-girlfriend in hospital.

They still fined him £156 with £25 costs and endorsed

his licence with the maximum six penalty points. For, as we have seen in **Police Cars and Other Emergency Service Vehicles**, the 1984 Road Traffic Regulation Act says that only vehicles being used 'for fire brigade, ambulance or police purposes' can legally exceed the speed limit. The rest of us must observe speed limits without question.

For instance, a thirty-nine-year-old sales manager motorist was stuck in a traffic jam on the M5 with his wife when he heard on the car telephone that his father-in-law was dying from a heart attack in hospital in Warwick. In the car in front were the West Midlands chief constable and his aide. He asked for their help. They gladly gave him a high-speed escort for so long as they were on the same road.

But minutes after they had parted, a policeman from another force booked him for doing just over 100 mph. His father-in-law had died by the time they got to the hospital but the Crown Prosecution Service, with its ineffable charm and sensitivity, still saw fit to prosecute. He was duly convicted and fined – but at least the Droitwich magistrates did not disqualify him.

It is even possible, as we have seen under **Breath Tests**, to avoid the normal consequences of a drink-driving conviction and keep your licence, if your hard-luck story (a) is genuine and (b) amounts to what the law calls a 'special reason'. But the judges have said that this must mean 'special to the offence and not the offender'.

The result is that motorists have saved their licence when driving a near-relative to hospital in a sudden medical emergency with no other vehicle available; where a car

was driven only 40 yards without causing danger in a
well-lit street at night, and where drink had without their
knowledge been laced with something stronger – but only
when they could prove they would otherwise have been
within the limit.

On the other hand, it will not help you to say that you
were only just over the limit and believed your driving
was unimpaired; or that your livelihood depended on your
keeping your licence; or that you had unwittingly drunk a
small amount of alcohol on an empty stomach.

There is a limit to the success rate of even the best
excuses, however genuine. A good example of this was a
case at Kingston upon Thames, Surrey, Magistrates' Court
in August 1996.

What had happened was that a thirty-eight-year-old
carpenter's van ran out of petrol on a stretch of dual
carriageway. The gauge showed empty and the vehicle
shuddered to a halt. But the driver was not too worried as
he knew that help was only minutes away. He played the
situation by the book: he switched on his warning lights
and used his mobile phone to call his business partner who
was travelling ten minutes behind and agreed to stop for
petrol. Also, the carpenter knew that his wife was due to
drive past soon and he was sure she would spot his
stranded vehicle. When a police patrol car came into view
and drew up beside him, he thought that they too might
be able to help – instead of which they reported him for
leaving his car on a road in a dangerous position, contrary
to Section 22 of the 1988 Road Traffic Act.

His hard-luck story had little effect upon the worthy

Kingston magistrates. Despite his plea of Not Guilty, they convicted him and fined him £40 plus £60 costs and gave him three penalty points. 'I was dealing with the situation as best I could. So why take me to court?' the angry motorist asked. A spokesman for the Crown Prosecution Service admitted that running out of petrol is not in itself an offence but, as a legal adviser to the AA commented, 'The police and courts do not accept that something like running out of petrol is a breakdown because it is self-induced.'

At times, I wonder if people in legal authority are 100 per cent human. Compassion is not their greatest characteristic.

Y

YELLOW LINES

As we all know, these are of two kinds: those painted along the road and those on the kerb. But not everyone knows that they have a different legal function.

When painted along the road, double yellow lines mean that 'waiting' – i.e. parking – is not allowed at any time. That is simple. But the situation gets unnecessarily complicated with single yellow lines. These mean that you can park at any time *except* within restricted hours and on certain days, usually Monday to Saturday but sometimes also on Sunday.

How do you know precisely which hours and days? Every controlled parking zone has its own details stated on 'time plates' displayed on poles at the entry to the zone. But, if restrictions differ in any specific street within that zone, there must be a different time plate *in that very street*. If no days are shown on the time plates, the restrictions are in force every day including Sunday and Bank Holidays.

The Highway Code states: 'Yellow lines can only give a guide to the restrictions and controls in force and signs, nearby or at a zone entry, must be consulted.' That is of course true, but it is easier and less hassle to find the nearest parking meter or pay-and-display ticket machine, where the relevant information is clearly stated.

Except on red lines along London's red routes, which we shall look at in a moment, you can always *briefly* pick up or drop off passengers even within restricted hours and days: that does not amount in law to breach of 'No Waiting' by-laws – you are not 'waiting' for anyone, simply dropping someone off. Furthermore, white bay markings on the road with upright signs alongside indicate where parking is specifically allowed within specified times.

The situation becomes more complicated with loading and unloading. This is where yellow lines painted along the kerb come in. They govern the situation. If there are none, it means there are no restrictions. If they are present, two lines mean no loading or unloading at any time whereas one line means not between the hours shown on the nearest time plate. But be careful. Stopping for permitted loading or unloading is not the same as stopping for quick shopping. The goods being loaded or unloaded must be of a type that cannot easily be carried to the vehicle by one person in one trip. 'They cannot be a fountain pen,' as a High Court judge once commented.

On some major roads in London, yellow lines have been replaced by red lines. These are the notorious 'red routes'. Red lines mean that you cannot stop to park, load or unload or even board or alight from a vehicle – except a licensed taxi or a car displaying an official Orange Badge for the disabled. As with yellow lines, single-line restrictions are shown on nearby signs, but double lines mean no stopping is allowed for whatever purpose at any time.

Yet even on red routes the authorities accept that a motor vehicle must sometimes be allowed to stop, however briefly. Red boxes on the road, with signs specifying the exact times allowed, indicate where you can park to load or unload. White boxes mean you can do so throughout the day.

For the sake of completeness, I should add that, as we have seen under **Excuses**, it is an offence to 'leave a motor vehicle in a dangerous position' (up to £1,000 fine, three penalty points and discretionary (but rare) disqualification) and to 'cause or permit an unnecessary obstruction' (up to £1,000 fine).

Z

ZEBRA CROSSINGS

Once someone steps on to a 'zebra', he has territorial immunity. Under Regulation 26 of the 1997 Zebra, Pelican and Puffin Pedestrian Crossings Regulations and General Directions, you must 'accord him precedence' if a pedestrian has stepped on to the crossing before your vehicle has arrived there. You must stop and let him pass, even if he put his foot on to the black and white stripes when your front wheels were already on the zigzag approach area. If not, you risk a fine of up to £1,000, three penalty points and (at least, in theory) a brief disqualification. Fortunately, the soft option of a £40 fixed penalty is available: usually if your speed was reasonable and the pedestrian gave you no chance to stop in time.

Each part of a crossing on either side of a central bollard, whether on a straight crossing or a staggered one, counts as a separate zebra and you cannot blithely assume that, because someone is in the process of using the zebra on one side of the bollard, you can safely proceed on your side. You should be wary that he might continue across.

Mr Justice Ormerod laid down in *Gibbons* v. *Kahl*, one of the earliest cases involving zebras to reach the courts back in 1955, only four years after zebra crossings were first painted on our roads: 'It is the duty of any motorist approaching such a crossing to do so in such a way that he can deal with the situation when he gets there. He must be in a position, and driving at such a speed, that if anybody is on the crossing he is in a position to stop. If he cannot see by reason of other traffic whether anybody is on the crossing or not, it is his duty to drive in such a way that he can stop if, in fact, there is somebody whose position on the crossing is masked by traffic.' That is still the law, and you cannot have anything more clear – or uncompromising.

We should all beware of misreading the scene and thinking that a pedestrian is letting us pass, 'waiving his precedence' as lawyers call it. If you are mistaken and the pedestrian does not really mean it, you still commit an offence. As Mr Justice Megaw ruled sternly in *Neal* v. Bedford in 1965, 'A motorist can only be certain of avoiding liability if he approaches the crossing at such a slow speed that he can stop in the event of any conceivable use of the crossing by any conceivable pedestrian except a suicidal one who deliberately walks in front of his car.' Such a last-minute crosser, if injured, would have his damages cut in a civil case because of his own 'contributory negligence' in not giving a motorist a reasonable chance of avoiding him, but the primary liability would still lie on the unfortunate driver.

Zebra crossings can even get a motorist into trouble as regards other drivers. If you see another driver who has stopped to allow a pedestrian to cross, you cannot pass him – even if no one has yet stepped on to the crossing or if he has already arrived safely on the opposite pavement. The mere fact that another driver has stopped 'for the purpose of complying with the Regulations' means that you also must do so, and I once myself unsuccessfully defended a motorist on just this charge.

If what I have written seems very 'heavy' and depressing, I have one word of comfort. Pedestrians can also fall foul of the Regulations – if they remain on a crossing 'longer than is necessary for the purpose of passing over it with reasonable despatch'. Then they too commit an offence and can be fined up to £400. But I have to tell you that I know of no reported case where this has actually happened.

ZERO TOLERANCE

Zero tolerance, that is to say, following the law to the letter, has never been part of our criminal law. If it were, the courts would be even more jammed than they already are and the system would quickly grind to a halt under the weight of its work-load. Discretion is an essential part of the administration of law. I have already quoted under **Must** Sir Hartley (now Lord) Shawcross, QC's, famous observation, when Attorney General, back in January 1951: 'It has never been the rule in this country – I hope it never will be – that suspected criminal offences must automatically be the subject of prosecution.'

But events in the summer of 2000 raised the interesting

question of whether zero tolerance specifically for speeding exists. The question arose after two surprising events that occurred in July that year.

The first surprise was that a senior Cabinet Minister, Jack Straw, could allow his Special Branch driver to drive him at 103 mph along the M5 near Taunton at 8.55 a.m. for no better reason than that he was late for an appointment with that other vociferous upholder of equality under the law, Tony Blair. What happened then was the absolute opposite of zero tolerance. For, when stopped by the police, Mr Straw's driver was not automatically given a fixed penalty notice (FPN) for his serious offence – as would have happened to any other motorist – but allowed to proceed calmly on his way.

To many less fortunate – or less highly placed – motorists the incident reeked of 'cover up' and hypocrisy. Few people will have disagreed with RAC Foundation spokesman Kevin Delaney's comment at the time: 'You cannot have two laws – one for the Home Secretary's police driver and another for everybody else.'

The second surprising event in that month was the issue by the ACPO of new guidelines to 'clarify' and 'toughen' its policy on enforcement of the speeding laws – several months before a lawsuit by the small lobby group Transport 2000 questioning ACPO's recent guidelines issued in February 2000 was due to reach the High Court. At first sight, it seemed a premature surrender by Norfolk Chief Constable Ken Williams, chairman of ACPO's traffic committee, in seeking to pre-empt the judges' eventual decision.

But, on closer inspection, the revised guidelines did not seem to amount to the 'U-turn' that Transport 2000 exultantly claimed. In fact, they were more of a compromise between the two extremes of zero tolerance and excessive laissez-faire. Mercifully, they were not an outright victory for Transport 2000.

In announcing the new guidelines, Chief Constable Williams made clear that the ACPO would give police officers greater discretion, not less. They would allow them to clamp down hard on those speeding in built-up areas, for example, while giving more leeway to drivers who are exceeding the limit on quiet roads at night.

Mr Williams said, 'Our guidance to chief constables on the prosecution of speeding offences has recently been enhanced to give proper emphasis to the important part that discretion plays within the decision-making processes of patrolling officers. As a result, the document now provides clearer guidance to police on the need for speeding offences to be strictly but fairly enforced and to the public on the risk of facing formal action at speeds very close to but above the speed limit.'

The earlier February 2000 guidelines undoubtedly gave the impression that drivers travelling at speeds below 'enforcement thresholds' specified by the ACPO would not be prosecuted. They stated: 'These thresholds are intended to strongly guide the use of police discretion.' An example was that a driver exceeding the 30-mph limit would be given the softer option of a fixed penalty notice (FPN) if he was travelling at 35 mph and would only receive a court summons if he was travelling at 50 mph.

But in July the ACPO claimed that it had never intended
to indicate 'that in all probability no action would be taken
below the threshold figures'. The new guidelines made
clear that anyone exceeding the thresholds would face
automatic action but officers could still use their discretion
in the 'gap' between the legal limits and the thresholds.
This exercise in semantics means that, if you are over the
threshold, you will almost certainly have a major problem.
If under the threshold but still illegal, you will have a
chance of avoiding prosecution – so be very polite to the
officer who stops you!

The moral is that nothing is written in stone. Zero
tolerance for those exceeding the limit does not exist. The
police do not automatically prosecute, even if there is no
doubt as to your guilt. But, on the other hand, you will still
be prosecuted if the justice of the case demands it – except,
of course, if you are a senior Cabinet Minister.

Useful Addresses

Association of British Insurers
51 Gresham Street
London EC2V 7HQ
Telephone 020 7600 3333

Automobile Association Legal
  Services
Lambert House
Stockport Road, Cheadle
Cheshire SK8 2DY
Telephone 0870 550 0600

British Parking Association
2 Clair Road,
Haywards Heath
West Sussex RH16 3DP
Telephone 01444 447 303

Camping and Caravanning Club
Greenfields House
Westwood Way
Coventry CV4 8JH
Telephone 02476 694995

Department of the Environment,
  Transport and the Regions
  (DETR)
Eland House
Bressenden Place
London SW1E 5DU
Telephone 020 7944 3000

Driver and Vehicle Licensing
  Agency (DVLA)
Swansea SA99 1BL
Telephone 01792 772 151
(Customer Enquiries Unit
Telephone 01792 772 134)

Driving Instructors Association,
Safety House,
Beddington Farm Road
Croydon, Surrey CR0 4XZ
Telephone 020 8665 5151

HPI (Car Fraud Detection
  Database)
Dolphin House
New Street
Salisbury
Wiltshire
Telephone 01722 422422

The Law Society
113 Chancery Lane
London WC2A 1PL
Telephone 020 7242 1222
Plus branches in local phone books.
Website: www.solicitors-online.com

Motor Insurers' Bureau
152 Silbury Boulevard
Central Milton Keynes MK9 1NB
Telephone 01908 240000

National Caravan Council
Catherine House
Victoria Road
Aldershot
Hampshire GU11 1SS
Telephone 01252 318251

The Pedestrians Association
3rd Floor, 31–33 Bondway
London SW8 1SJ
Telephone 020 7820 1010

RAC Legal Services
PO Box 700
Bristol BS99 1RB
Telephone 01454 208000

RAC Motoring Services
Great Park Road
Bradley Stoke
Bristol BS32 4QN
Telephone 01454 208000

Royal Society for the Prevention of
  Accidents (ROSPA)
ROSPA House, Edgbaston Park
353 Bristol Road
Birmingham B5 7ST
Telephone 0121 248 2000